Table of Contents

IV

V

VI

Practice Examinations

Introduction

The AP Biology exam tests a student on knowledge from an introductory level college biology class. The exam changed in 2012 to a different format. Now, the exam consists of 63 multiple-choice questions with four answer options, 6 grid-in questions and 8 free-response questions. This is different from previous exams in which there were 100 multiple-choice questions. The new exam tests more difficult content and interpretation of figures and graphs more extensively, compared to the easier multiple-choice questions found on the old exam.

Exam Question Formats

1. *Multiple Choice*: A question with four answer choices. The question may contain a figure or a chart to assist in answering the question. Points are not deducted for a wrong answer, so feel free to guess on questions that you don't know the answer to.

2. *Grid-In Questions*: A question will be asked that possesses a numerical answer. The answer will be gridded, or bubbled in, onto your answer sheet. Make sure to use appropriate rounding when answering these questions.

3. *Free-Response Questions*: There are two long-answer free-response questions and six short answer free response questions. Make sure to address every point that the exam requires. There is no penalty for length on these questions, but incorrect information will result in a loss of points (so don't include irrelevant information!

What's the Big Idea?

Actually, there are four "Big Ideas" tested on the exam:

1. Evolution and Natural Selection
2. Production and use of energy at the cellular Level
3. Cellular signaling and transport
4. Interaction of Biological Systems

These four primary areas contain information on a range of topics, including:

- Chemistry

- Cells

- Respiration

- Photosynthesis

- DNA and Molecular Genetics

- Evolution

- Heredity

- Ecology and Biological Diversity

- Plant Characteristics

- Animal Characteristics

- Animal Behavior.

This guide will provide an overview of the most important topics within each of these study areas.

I

Introduction to Chemistry

The Periodic Table

The periodic table contains information on the known elements. Each element is a pure chemical substance that can be used to form molecules and compounds. Elements are distinguished by the number of protons they possess. The atomic number of each element refers to the number of protons contained in the nucleus of that element. For example, Carbon has an atomic number of 6, meaning that it has six protons in its nucleus.

hydrogen 1 H 1.0079																	helium 2 He 4.0026
lithium 3 Li 6.941	beryllium 4 Be 9.0122											boron 5 B 10.811	carbon 6 C 12.011	nitrogen 7 N 14.007	oxygen 8 O 15.999	fluorine 9 F 18.998	neon 10 Ne 20.180
sodium 11 Na 22.990	magnesium 12 Mg 24.305											aluminium 13 Al 26.982	silicon 14 Si 28.086	phosphorus 15 P 30.974	sulfur 16 S 32.065	chlorine 17 Cl 35.453	argon 18 Ar 39.948
potassium 19 K 39.098	calcium 20 Ca 40.078	scandium 21 Sc 44.956	titanium 22 Ti 47.867	vanadium 23 V 50.942	chromium 24 Cr 51.996	manganese 25 Mn 54.938	iron 26 Fe 55.845	cobalt 27 Co 58.933	nickel 28 Ni 58.693	copper 29 Cu 63.546	zinc 30 Zn 65.39	gallium 31 Ga 69.723	germanium 32 Ge 72.61	arsenic 33 As 74.922	selenium 34 Se 78.96	bromine 35 Br 79.904	krypton 36 Kr 83.80
rubidium 37 Rb 85.468	strontium 38 Sr 87.62	yttrium 39 Y 88.906	zirconium 40 Zr 91.224	niobium 41 Nb 92.906	molybdenum 42 Mo 95.94	technetium 43 Tc [98]	ruthenium 44 Ru 101.07	rhodium 45 Rh 102.91	palladium 46 Pd 106.42	silver 47 Ag 107.87	cadmium 48 Cd 112.41	indium 49 In 114.82	tin 50 Sn 118.71	antimony 51 Sb 121.76	tellurium 52 Te 127.60	iodine 53 I 126.90	xenon 54 Xe 131.29
caesium 55 Cs 132.91	barium 56 Ba 137.33	57-70 *	lutetium 71 Lu 174.97	hafnium 72 Hf 178.49	tantalum 73 Ta 180.95	tungsten 74 W 183.84	rhenium 75 Re 186.21	osmium 76 Os 190.23	iridium 77 Ir 192.22	platinum 78 Pt 195.08	gold 79 Au 196.97	mercury 80 Hg 200.59	thallium 81 Tl 204.38	lead 82 Pb 207.2	bismuth 83 Bi 208.98	polonium 84 Po [209]	astatine 85 At [210]	radon 86 Rn [222]
francium 87 Fr [223]	radium 88 Ra [226]	89-102 **	lawrencium 103 Lr [262]	rutherfordium 104 Rf [261]	dubnium 105 Db [262]	seaborgium 106 Sg [266]	bohrium 107 Bh [264]	hassium 108 Hs [269]	meitnerium 109 Mt [268]	ununnilium 110 Uun [271]	unununium 111 Uuu [272]	ununbium 112 Uub [277]		ununquadium 114 Uuq [289]				

*Lanthanide series	lanthanum 57 La 138.91	cerium 58 Ce 140.12	praseodymium 59 Pr 140.91	neodymium 60 Nd 144.24	promethium 61 Pm [145]	samarium 62 Sm 150.36	europium 63 Eu 151.96	gadolinium 64 Gd 157.25	terbium 65 Tb 158.93	dysprosium 66 Dy 162.50	holmium 67 Ho 164.93	erbium 68 Er 167.26	thulium 69 Tm 168.93	ytterbium 70 Yb 173.04
**Actinide series	actinium 89 Ac [227]	thorium 90 Th 232.04	protactinium 91 Pa 231.04	uranium 92 U 238.03	neptunium 93 Np [237]	plutonium 94 Pu [244]	americium 95 Am [243]	curium 96 Cm [247]	berkelium 97 Bk [247]	californium 98 Cf [251]	einsteinium 99 Es [252]	fermium 100 Fm [257]	mendelevium 101 Md [258]	nobelium 102 No [259]

The periodic table can be used to understand the general properties of elements. Elements in the first two columns are the alkaline earth metals, and are quite reactive. Elements from column 3 to 11 are the metals, and are able to interact in many different reactions. The elements in column 18, the last column on the right, are noble gases, and have very low reactivity due to their full electron shell.

Elements increase in electronegativity as they approach the upper right of the periodic table. Elements in this part of the table, such as fluorine and chlorine, are extremely reactive, especially with alkaline earth metals.

The most common elements found on earth are carbon, nitrogen, oxygen and hydrogen, which form the building blocks of much of the proteins, sugars, and fats contained in living organisms. The air that we breathe is approximately 21% oxygen and 77% nitrogen, with the remaining 2% made up of a mixture of carbon dioxide, noble gases and methane.

Bonds

A bond is an interaction between the electrons of two atoms. An atom consists of a nucleus of protons and neutrons surrounded by a shell of electrons. The interaction between these electrons causes a bond to form. You need to know three major types of bonds:

- *Ionic* – A polar bond is formed because of the difference in charge between two atoms, when electrons transfer from one atom to another. A standard example of an ionic bond is the one formed between sodium and chlorine, into table salt, NaCl. The sodium atom has one electron in its valence shell, and the chlorine atom has seven. All atoms seek out a full valence shell. To do this, sodium will lose one electron, and give it to chlorine. As a result, we get the ions Na^+ and Cl^-. Due to the opposite charge of these two ions, they will form an ionic bond together. Other examples of molecules that contain an ionic bond are magnesium chloride ($MgCl_2$), calcium oxide (CaO), and hydrogen chloride (HCl).

- *Covalent* – A covalent bond is formed when electrons are shared between the two atoms. Note that there is no such thing as a true covalent bond; the majority of bonds have both ionic and covalent nature. The best way to recognize a covalent bond is when the two atoms are close in electronegativity. The majority of gases, such as O_2, N_2, and CO_2, are all formed through a covalent bond interaction.

- *Hydrogen Bond* – Hydrogen bonds are formed through weak polar interactions between molecules that contain atoms with a large difference in electronegativity. A classic example is the water molecule, as seen below:

Due to the high electronegativity of the oxygen atom, electrons will be pulled away from the bond between hydrogen and oxygen. This will result in a net positive dipole for the hydrogen atom and a net negative dipole for the oxygen. As a result, when water molecules come into contact with one another, they form hydrogen bonds between the positive and negative charges located on each molecule.

Properties of Water

The hydrogen bonding properties of water give it some very unique characteristics that are essential for life. These properties include:

- *High adhesive and cohesion properties* – water molecules stick to each other, forming the basis for the capillary action effect that moves water from the roots up to the leaves in plants.

- *Polar qualities* – The polarity of water means that many other substances are soluble in water, making it ideal as a solution to sustain life.

- *High heat capacity* – The high heat capacity of water is about 4.2 J/g*K, which is one of the highest of any materials. This heat capacity provides a buffer against rapid temperature changes. The large bodies of water on Earth are able to absorb or lose significant amounts of energy without a drastic change in temperature.

Acids, Bases and pH

The pH of a solution is related to the concentration of hydrogen ions in a solution. It is different from the pKa of a compound, which is related to the dissociation constant of an acid or base. The pH of a solution is calculated according to the following equation:

$$pH = -\log[H^+] \qquad\qquad [H^+] = 10^{-pH}$$

This equation can be used to find the pH of a solution given the concentration of hydrogen ions, or can be used to find the concentration of hydrogen ions given the pH. A low pH is acidic, a pH of 7 is neutral (water), and a pH of 14 is basic. Below is a table of some common compounds and their pH at 0.1 molarity:

Compound	pH at 0.1M in water
Hydrogen Chloride	1.0
Acetic Acid	2.87
Ammonium Hydroxide	11.13

An important thing to remember is that pH is a logarithmic scale. Thus, a pH of 1 is 10 times stronger than a pH of 2. Likewise, a pH of 10 has 10 times more basic ions than a pH of 9.

Organic Molecules

There are several classes of organic compounds commonly found in living organisms. These include sugars/carbohydrates, proteins, and lipids. Combined, these three classes of compounds make up more than 95% of non-water material in living organisms.

Organic compounds, specifically, are those that contain carbon. These compounds, such as glucose, triacylglycerol and guanine, are usually found and used in day-to-day metabolic processes. Inorganic compounds are those that do not contain carbon. These make up a very small fraction of mass in living organisms, and are usually minerals such as potassium, sodium, and iron.

Sugars/Carbohydrates

Carbohydrate compounds are molecules made of carbon, hydrogen, and oxygen. Sugars are primarily used in organisms as a source of energy. They can catabolize using an oxidation process to create energy molecules such as adenosine triphosphate (ATP) or Nicotinamide adenine dinucleotide (NAD+), providing a source of electrons to drive cellular processes.

The basic formula for a carbohydrate is CH_2O, and the majority of carbohydrates are multiples of this empirical formula. For example, glucose is $C_6H_{12}O_6$.

Carbohydrates can bond together to form polymeric compounds. Some polymers of glucose include starch and cellulose. Starch is an energy molecule used to store excess sugar, and cellulose is a support fiber responsible in part for the strength of plants.

Lipids

Lipids are compounds primarily composed of carbon and hydrogen, with a small percentage of atoms being oxygen. Lipids contain a 'head', usually formed of glycerol or phosphate, and a 'tail', which is a hydrocarbon chain. An example of a free fatty acid lipid is seen below:

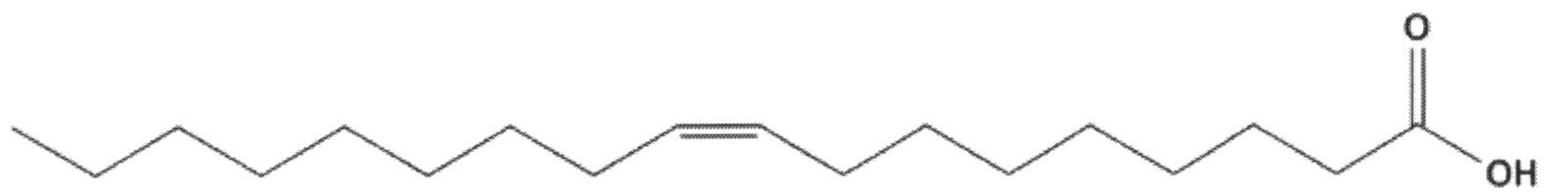

There are three important components of a lipid:

- *Head* – The composition of the head, whether it is a carboxylic acid functional group, a phosphate group, or some other functional group, is usually polar, meaning it is hydrophilic.

- *Tail* – The tail is composed of carbon and hydrogen, and is usually nonpolar, meaning it is hydrophobic.

- *Saturation* – The number of double bonds in the tail of the lipid affects its steric interactions. The more double bonds a lipid tail has, the more unsaturated the molecule is, and the more bends there are in its structure. As a result, unsaturated fats tend to solidify at room temperature, whereas saturated fats are liquid at room temperature.

The combined polarity of the lipid head and the non-polarity of the lipid tail is a unique feature of lipids critical to the formation of the phospholipid bilayer, seen in the cell membrane. The fatty acid tails are all pointed inward, and the heads are pointed outward. This provides a semi-permeable membrane that allows a cell to separate its contents from the environment.

Proteins

Proteins are large molecules composed of a long chain of amino acids. The sequence of the amino acid chain determines the protein's structure and function.

The amino acid is composed of three parts:

- Amino group – The amino group is –NH2, and is seen on all amino acids

- Carboxyl group – The carboxyl group is –COOH, and is seen on all amino acids

- R group – The R-group is a unique functional group that is different for each amino acid. For example, in the histidine amino acid seen below, the R group is a cyclic imidazole group.

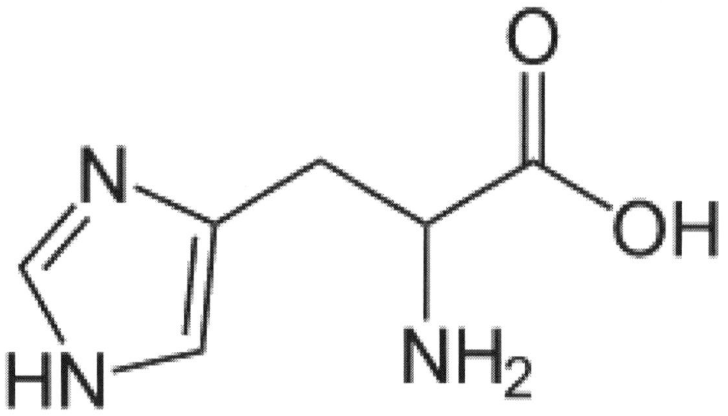

The R-group determines the amino acid's physiological function. For example, the imidazole group gives histidine a pH of around 7, which makes histidine a very important amino acid to humans, since our bodies function around a pH of 7.

There are 22 amino acids used in the building blocks for life. It is not important to know what each of these amino acids are, but it is important to know that sequences of these amino acids form proteins, and that each amino acid has a unique R-functional group.

The cell is the lowest unit of life; all higher organisms are composed of cells. Cells can be anywhere between 20 µm to 100 µm in size, and sometimes even larger. Cells were first discovered by the Englishman Robert Hooke, the inventor of the microscope, in the 1600s. However, cell theory truly began to develop when a Dutchman named Antony van Leeuwenhoek pioneered new developments in the field of microscopy, allowing scientists to view bacteria, protozoa and other microorganisms.

Cell Subgroups

Cells are roughly divided into two large subgroups: Prokaryotic cells and Eukaryotic cells. The primary similarities and differences are listed below:

Similarities between Prokaryotic and Eukaryotic Cells

- Both cells have cell membranes and often have cell walls.
- Both types of cell can have the following general cell structures:
  - Mitochondria
  - Ribosome
  - Vacuole
  - Flagella
- Both types of cell contain DNA and RNA

Traits Unique to Prokaryotic Cells

- Prokaryotic cells, which contain bacteria, are the only types of cells, which contain peptidoglycan, a sugar, and amino acid layer that supports the cell membrane.
- Prokaryotic cells do not have a nuclear membrane.
- Many prokaryotic cells contain plasmids, which are circular rings of DNA that hold genetic information.

Traits Unique to Eukaryotic Cells

- Eukaryotic cells have a nuclear membrane, and DNA is contained within the membrane.

- Eukaryotic cells have a Golgi body, which is used for transport of proteins.

- Some Eukaryotic cells have lysosomes or peroxisomes, which are used in digestion.

Parts of the Cell

Although the cell is the smallest unit of life, there are many small bodies, called organelles, which exist in the cell to perform certain functions. These organelles are required for a variety of cell functions, and in some cases, even have their own DNA. The most important organelles are:

- *Mitochondria* – The mitochondria are the organelles responsible for making ATP within the cell. A mitochondria has several layers of membranes used to assist the electron transport pathway. This pathway uses energy provided by molecules such as glucose or fat (lipid) to generate ATP through the transfer of electrons to the ATP molecule.

- *Vacuole* – A vacuole is a small body used to transfer materials within and out of the cell. It has a membrane of its own and can carry things such as cell wastes, sugars or proteins.

- *Nucleus* – The nucleus of a cell (only a eukaryotic cell), contains all of its genetic information in the form of DNA. In the nucleus, DNA replication and transcription occurs. In the eukaryotic cell, after transcription, the mRNA is exported out of the nucleus into the cytosol for use.

- *Endoplasmic reticulum* – The ER, for short, is used for translation of mRNA into proteins, and for the transport of proteins out of the cell. The rough endoplasmic reticulum has many ribosomes attached to it, which function as the cell's machinery in transforming RNA into protein.

- *Ribosome* – The ribosome is a small two-protein unit that reads mRNA, and with the assistance of transport proteins, creates an amino acid.

Cell Membrane

The cell membrane is a unique layer that performs numerous functions, and is composed of a compound type called a phospholipid, as seen below:

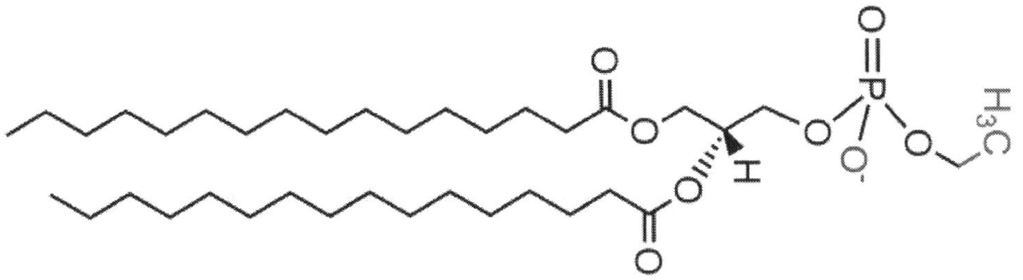

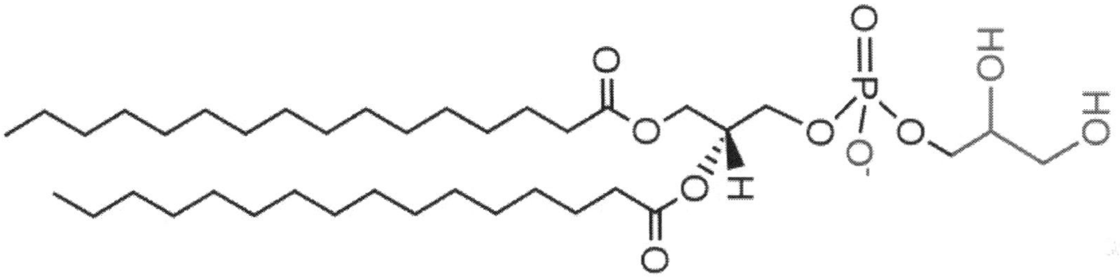

These phospholipid compounds are amphipathic, and consist of an alkane tail and a phospho-group head. The alkane lipid tail is hydrophobic, meaning it will not allow water to pass through, and the phosphate group head is hydrophilic, which allows water to pass through. The arrangement of these molecules forms a bilayer, which has a hydrophobic middle layer. In this manner, the cell is able to control the import and export of various substances into the cell. An example of a phospholipid bilayer is seen on the next page:

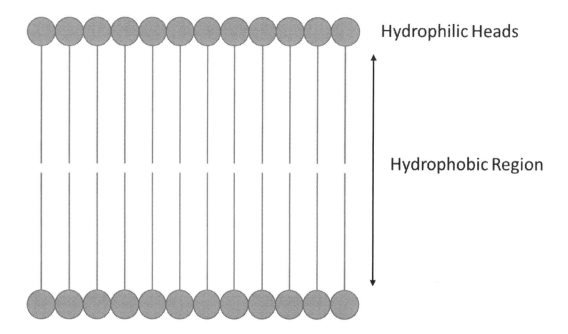

Hydrophilic Heads

Hydrophobic Region

In addition to the phospholipid bilayer, the cell membrane often includes proteins, which perform a variety of functions. Some proteins are used as receptors, which allow the cell to interact with its surroundings. Others are transmembrane proteins, meaning that they cross the entire membrane. These types of proteins are usually channels, which allow the transportation of molecules into and out of the cell.

Finally, membrane proteins are also used in cell-to-cell interaction. This includes functions such as cell-cell joining or recognition, in which a cell membrane protein contacts a protein from another cell. A good example of this is the immune response in the human body. Due to the proteins found on the cell membrane of antigens, immune system cells can contact, recognize and attempt to remove them.

Membrane Transport

A cell needs to be able to obtain nutrients and vitamins from outside the cell membrane, while at the same time preventing harmful toxins or species from entering the cell. Two major classes of transportation occur across the cell wall:

1. *Active transport*: This type of transport requires the use of energy molecules, such as ATP, to facilitate the transportation of a molecule across the cell membrane.

2. *Passive transport*: This type of transport does not require energy, and allows molecules such as water to passively diffuse across the cell membrane.

The balance of water in the cell is one of the most important regulatory mechanisms for the cell. Water enters or exits the cell through a process called osmosis. This movement of water does not usually require energy, and the movement is regulated by a factor called *tonicity*.

Tonicity is the concentration of solutes in the cell. Solutes can be salt ions, such as sodium or chlorine, or other molecules such as sugar, amino acids, or proteins. The difference in tonicity between the cell and its outside environment governs the transportation of water into and out of the cell. For example, if there is a higher tonicity inside the cell, then water will enter the cell. If there is a higher tonicity outside the cell, the water will leave the cell. This is due to the idea that there is a driving force called a chemiosmotic potential that attempts to make tonicity equal across a membrane.

In the example below, the cell has a concentration of solutes of 80 mM, and the outside environment has a concentration of solutes of 40 mM. Where will the water go?

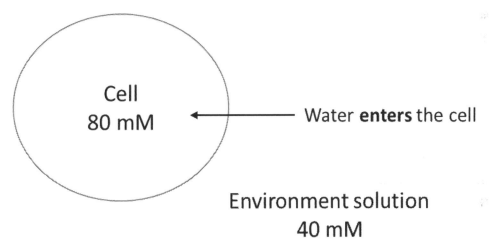

In this case, water will enter the cell until the concentration of solutes in the cell matches the concentration of solutes in the environment. This will cause the cell to swell in size. There are three terms to know when working with tonicity:

- *Isotonic* – An isotonic cell has the same concentration of solutes inside and outside of the cell. There will be no transport of water in this case.

- *Hypertonic* – A hypertonic cell has a lower concentration of solutes inside than outside of the cell. The cell will lose water to the environment and shrivel. This is what happens if you put a cell into a salty solution.

- *Hypotonic* – A hypotonic cell has a higher concentration of solutes inside than outside of the cell. The cell will absorb water from the environment and swell, becoming turgid.

Facilitated Diffusion

Facilitated diffusion is a form of passive transport that does not require energy. However, it does require the use of proteins located on the cell membrane. These transport proteins typically have a "channel" running through the core of a protein specific to a certain type of molecule. For example, a transport protein for sodium only allows sodium to flow through the channel.

Active Transport

Active transport uses ATP to accomplish one of two tasks. Active transport can move an ion against the concentration gradient (from low concentration to high), or it can be used to import or export a bulky molecule, such as a sugar or a protein, across the cell membrane.

Active transport also requires the use of proteins. ATP produced by the cell binds to the proteins in the cell membrane and is hydrolyzed, producing the energy required to change the conformational structure of the protein. This change in the structure of the protein allows the protein to funnel molecules across the cell membrane.

Enzymes are an important type of protein crucial for aiding various reactions in the cell. An enzyme is a large protein that acts as a catalyst. A catalyst is a substance able to speed up a reaction through:

- Reducing the activation energy of a reaction

- Bringing reactants closer together

All chemical reactions have something called an activation energy. This is the amount of energy required before a reaction can begin. For some reactions, this barrier is quite high at room temperature, and this is where enzymes come in.

- *Function: reducing activation energy* – Enzymes can reduce the activation energy of a reaction through interaction with the bonds in the reactants. Many enzymes have something called an "active site", which is an area of the protein that has certain functional groups able to bind with a reactant. This binding forms a stabilized intermediate that allows the reactant to more easily dissociate or react with another reagent.

- *Function: bringing reactants closer together* – Many reaction rates are limited by the concentration of reactants in the solution. For example, in a cell, the concentration of glucose is usually less than 0.5 mM. This means that the chance for a glucose molecule to contact another reactant is quite low. Enzymes can bind to a glucose molecule, for example, and then bind to the other reactant, forcing the reaction to take place.

Enzymes are unique proteins that have a specific active site. They only react with the chemical that they were designed for or, in some cases, other substrates that have very similar structures. Some examples of important enzymes include:

- *DNA polymerase*: the enzyme responsible for copying DNA. The enzyme binds to a single strand of DNA and assembles nucleotides to match the strand.

- *Pyruvate kinase*: the enzyme responsible for glycolysis, which is the initial breakdown of glucose in the human body (and other organisms).

- *Endoglucanase*: enzyme responsible for the breakdown of cellulose in fungi and bacteria. This enzyme breaks down the cellulose chain into smaller sugars for use.

Cellular Metabolism

Metabolism is the process of converting molecules into energy or other molecules necessary to sustain life. Imagine a cell as a small chemical factory that takes in nutrients from the outside and is able to convert these nutrients into more useful compounds. This process can be best understood as a pathway:

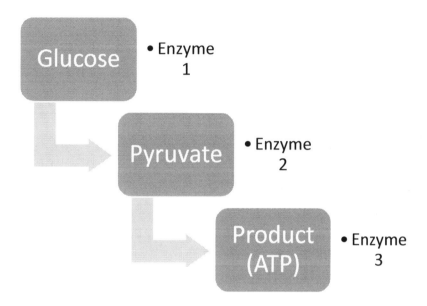

In the example above, which is simplified, a glucose molecule is converted into an intermediate, pyruvate, and finally into a product, in this case ATP. In a single cell, there are hundreds if not thousands of these metabolic pathways that all function to keep the cell alive.

Catabolism

A major function of metabolism is catabolism, which is the breakdown of molecules. A catabolic pathway takes a larger molecule and transforms it into either something smaller or into energy. The example shown above of the breakdown of glucose is a catabolic pathway.

Anabolism

Anabolism is the opposite of catabolism. In an anabolic pathway, energy and smaller molecules are used by the cell in order to build a more complicated molecule, such as a protein. A good example of an anabolic pathway would be the synthesis of a protein.

ATP: The Most Important Energy Molecule

ATP is short for adenosine triphosphate, and is the most common energy molecule. The ATP molecule is formed from ribose, a sugar, and contains three phosphate groups. ATP is primarily used for energy, but is also used to form adenine, which is a nucleoside   used in the construction of both DNA and RNA.

ATP is able to store energy through the formation of high-energy bonds between the phosphate groups in the "tail" of the molecule. When the last phosphate bond in the group is broken through a hydrolysis reaction, a phosphate molecule is released. This exothermic reaction releases energy that can then be used to drive a different cellular reaction. The product of the reaction is a phosphate molecule, and a lower energy ADP molecule. ADP needs to be recycled by the cell to form ATP again for further use. This process of forming ATP is a catabolic process that largely occurs in the mitochondria. The energy to reform ATP in the human body can be derived from three primary sources: lipids, proteins, and carbohydrates.

ATP is produced through a process called catabolism, which can take place in one of two ways. The first method, in which oxygen is used, is called a respiratory pathway. In a respiratory pathway, a food substance, such as glucose or amino acids, is broken down with the use of oxygen, and ATP is gained. The second method, which will be addressed in the next section, is an anaerobic process that does not use oxygen called fermentation.

The basic overall process of aerobic respiration is as follows:

$$Organic\ Compound + Oxygen \rightarrow Carbon\ Dioxide + Water + Energy$$

As a result, animals (and humans) that use aerobic respiration require oxygen to live. We breathe in oxygen using our lungs for respiration, and produce carbon dioxide and water as a byproduct.

The energy obtained from the breakdown of organic compounds is due to energy held within the bonds of the compound. This energy can vary widely, from about four kcal of energy per gram of carbohydrate to nine kcal per gram of fat, or lipid. The transfer of energy from the bonds breaking in these molecules occurs through an oxidation-reduction reaction, which involves the transfer of electrons from one species to another.

In respiration, there are two primary pathways you need to know for the examination. The first is glycolysis, which breaks down glucose into two molecules of pyruvate, and produces a little ATP. The second is the citric acid cycle, which takes pyruvate and produces much more ATP, as well as the associated byproduct of carbon dioxide.

Glycolysis

Glycolysis is the first step in the breakdown of sugars. The overall reaction of glycolysis is as follows:

$$\text{Glucose} + 2\,[NAD]^+ + 2\,[ADP] + 2\,[P]_i \xrightarrow{\hspace{2cm}} 2\ \text{Pyruvate} + 2\,[NADH] + 2\,H^+ + 2\,[ATP] + 2\,H_2O$$

Overall, a glucose molecule is used to produce two pyruvate molecules, which are fed into the citric acid cycle, and four energy molecules: two NADH and two ATP molecules, as well as two molecules of water.

The conversion of glucose into these products takes place over a ten- step pathway, which involves two phases. The first phase uses energy in order to break apart the glucose molecule. The second phase then recovers energy in the form of ATP and NADH, and results in the production of the pyruvate molecules.

Not all of the steps are covered in this guide, but the steps that use and produce energy are listed below:

Energy Consuming Steps

- Glucose + ATP → Glucose-6-phosphate + ADP

- Fructose 6-phosphate + ATP → Fructose 1,6-bisphosphate + AdP

Energy Releasing Steps

These reactions each happen twice, once for each molecule of pyruvate:

- Glyceraldehyde 3-phosphate + NAD+ → 1,3-bisphosphoglycerate + NADH

- 1,3-bisphosphoglycerate + ADP → 3-phosphoglycerate + ATP

- Phosphoenolpyruvate + ADP → Pyruvate + ATP

As a result, there is a net production of four molecules of ATP and two molecules of NADH. There is a corresponding use of two molecules of ATP. This results in the net production of two ATP, two NADH and two pyruvate molecules.

Citric Acid Cycle

The majority of the energy in the glucose molecule has not been released by glycolysis, however. The next step, the citric acid cycle, will produce the bulk of the ATP that can be derived from glucose. The citric acid cycle, if operating at full efficiency, can produce 38 molecules of ATP - over ten times the net ATP gain seen in glycolysis.

In eukaryotic cells, the citric acid cycle takes place in the mitochondria of the cell. The same reaction can occur in the cytosol/cytoplasm of prokaryotic cells. The citric acid cycle gets its name from the production and re-absorption of citric acid during the process. During the course of the TCA cycle, a molecule of pyruvate derived from glycolysis is transformed into three molecules of CO_2 and about 16 molecules of ATP. The TCA cycle needs to run twice for each molecule of glucose, due to the two molecules of pyruvate obtained from a molecule of glucose.

Roughly, ten steps occur in the citric acid cycle. They are summarized in the list below:

1. Pyruvate is oxidized by Coenzyme A. One NADH is produced as well as a CO_2 molecule, and the product, Acetyl-CoA.

2. Acetyl-CoA + Oxaloacetate produces a citrate molecule.

3. Citrate is converted to iso-citrate through the removal of a water molecule.

4. Iso-citrate is oxidized by oxygen, releasing carbon dioxide.

5. Iso-citrate is reduced by NAD+, forming NADH and alpha-ketoglutarate

6. Alpha-ketoglutarate is oxidized by oxygen, creating another molecule of NADH and Succinyl CoA.

7. Succyinl CoA is used to produce ATP and a molecule of succinate.

8. Succinate is converted to fumarate, forming another energy molecule, $FADH_2$.

9. Fumarate reacts with water to form malate, or malic acid.

10. Malate is reduced by NAD+ to form oxaloacetate, the starting reagent, and another molecule of NADH.

- In each cycle of the citric acid cycle, three NADH and one $FADH_2$ are produced. These molecules are used to feed the electron transport pathway, which makes ATP.

- The TCA cycle produces three molecules of carbon dioxide from the starting pyruvate molecule.

- Each glucose molecule requires two cycles of the citric acid cycle.

Electron Transport Pathway

The electron transport pathway is located in the mitochondria in the eukaryotic cell. In the pathway, a series of electron carries takes electrons from energy molecules produced by catabolism and uses them to generate ATP. The source of these electrons is usually NADH and $FADH_2$ generated from the citric acid cycle. These compounds can react in the following manner to donate electrons:

$$NADH \rightarrow NAD^+ + H^+ + 2e-$$

In this way, each NADH molecule can donate two electrons and each $FADH_2$ molecule can donate four electrons. The energy gained from the electrons is used by ATP synthase to create ATP from ADP. The ATP synthase uses the chemiosmotic potential of the increased hydrogen ions produced by the dissociation of the energy molecules to work as a sort of pump. The flow of the hydrogen ions through the ATP synthase molecules provides the energy to generate ATP.

Key Facts to Remember About the Electron Transport Chain

- The Electron Transport Chain itself does not generate ATP. Instead, it creates a concentration of hydrogen ions on one side of the mitochondrial membrane.

- The hydrogen ions are then pumped through ATP synthase to create ATP.

The efficiency of aerobic respiration in energy generation is remarkably high. A mole (180 grams) of glucose, if burned, will release about 686 kcal of energy. On the other hand, if consumed by a human and used in respiration, we can store about 234 kcal of that energy in the form of ATP. This is a net efficiency of about 34%. In comparison, using fuel in a car can generate an average of only 22% of useable energy, meaning the remainder of the energy is released as heat or other compounds by the car.

Fermentation is an alternative process that can generate ATP in anaerobic organisms. An anaerobic organism does not need oxygen to live. The best example is yeast. Yeast can live without oxygen, and are known to ferment sugars, producing ethanol and carbon dioxide, which is the source of the carbonation for beer. There are two primary forms of fermentation, alcohol and lactic acid fermentation.

Alcohol Fermentation

Alcohol fermentation is probably the most common type. After glycolysis occurs, the pyruvate is converted into ethanol. 2-NADH is used in the process, but as acetaldehyde is converted into ethanol, 2-NADH is produced.

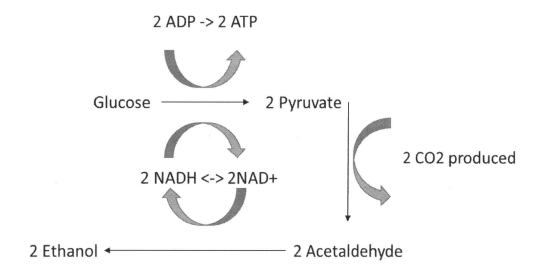

Lactic Acid Fermentation

Lactic acid fermentation differs only slightly from alcohol fermentation. Instead of acetaldehyde being produced, the pyruvate is directly fermented into lactic acid. This takes place in some fungi and bacteria, and can occur in the human body. When you use up your excess stores of ATP during strenuous exercise, and the citric acid cycle is unable to provide more ATP quickly, lactic acid fermentation occurs in your body to produce additional energy. However, the lactic acid in your muscles will cause a "burning" feeling.

II

Introduction to Plants

Plants are unique organisms that make up the largest percentage of organic matter on the planet. Without plants, which are autotrophs, the majority of other living organisms could not exist. Plants provide both a valuable source of oxygen and nutrients, due to their production of sugars from photosynthesis.

A plant is composed of three basic units:

- *Roots* – The roots of plants reside in the soil, and are responsible for absorbing water and minerals from the soil. There are two types of roots: a taproot, which is a central, thick root (think of a carrot), and lateral roots, which are smaller roots that branch out from the main root.

- *Stem*/Shoot – The stem of the plant provides structural stability. The stem also moves water from the roots to all other parts of the plant.

- *Leaf* – The leaf of the plant is high in surface area and contains the majority of the chlorophyll. The leaves absorb sunlight and perform photosynthesis.

The Vascular Tissue System

Vascular tissue is able to transport sugar and water to other parts of the plant. This is a vital process. In plants, there are two types of vascular tissue: Phloem and Xylem. Xylem is commonly known as woody tissue, and is very stiff. It consists of a series of hollow cell structures that move water from the roots up to the leaves or flowers. Phloem is a living tissue near the outside of the stem of the plant, and transports sugars. In addition to these two types of cells, there are three major types of plant cells in the leaves:

1. *Parenchyma* – The parenchyma cells have thin, flexible cell walls and have a large vacuole in the middle of the cell used for storage. These types of cells perform many functions, including many metabolic reactions. The interior of leaves contain parenchyma cells, and most fruit tissue is made of parenchyma cells.

2. *Collenchyma* – The collenchyma cells are seen in parts of the stem and support the plant as it is growing. These cells remain flexible even as they get older.

3. *Sclerenchyma* – The sclerenchyma cells are the most rigid of the cells. These cell types contain a lot of lignin and cellulose in the secondary cell wall, making it an indigestible structural component of the plant. Once mature, sclerenchyma cells are no longer flexible and cannot move.

Growth of Roots

The roots grow starting at the root meristem, which is an area of quickly dividing cells. In this area, new root cells are created, and are capped by a harder layer of tissue known as the root cap. The tissue of the roots is primarily parenchyma cells, which can store water and nutrients. Additionally, some root tubers, such as potatoes and carrots, are able to elongate and store significant amounts of nutrients.

Growth of Shoots

Shoots also start growth from a meristem, but this is known as a shoot apical meristem. When a leaf bud starts developing, a small bud known as a primordia leaf forms. As the leaf shoot develops, it may branch out.

Leaf Structure

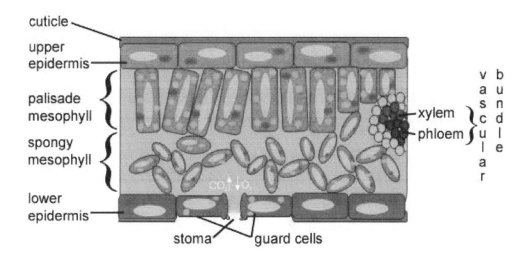

The figure above presents the general structure of a leaf. The epidermis is the outer layer of leaf cells, and is surrounded by a layer called the cuticle. The cuticle is a waxy layer that aids the plant in retaining moisture. This layer helps to prevent evaporation of water from the plant leaf. The epidermis also contains structures called stomata (singular: stoma). These openings in the leaf structure allow carbon dioxide and oxygen to be exchanged. Recall that photosynthesis produces oxygen, and requires carbon dioxide.

In the middle of the leaf are the two types of mesophyll, the palisade and spongy mesophyll. The mesophyll consists of parenchyma type cells that contain a lot of chlorophyll. These cells are specialized for photosynthesis. The palisade mesophyll has layers of parallel cells and is located on the upper portion of the leaf.

The spongy mesophyll is a collection of loosely organized cells that have many spaces in which carbon dioxide and oxygen are able to penetrate. This organization allows for CO2 and O2 to exchange from the palisade mesophyll section.

The Cambium Layer

The cambium layer of cells is a circle of high growth cells on the outer edge of the stem. The cambium is responsible for the majority of growth in trees. Damaging the cambium layer can greatly injure a tree's ability to grow, so human beings should take care not to damage a tree's bark.

Transpiration in Plants

In plants, the movement of water from the roots to the top of the plant is an important and difficult process. Diffusion is effective over short distances, but in order to move water to the top of a 20-meter tall tree, additional forces are needed.

In plants, the bulk flow of water from the roots is regulated by several mechanisms. These include the capillary action of water moving up the xylem, the respiration of water from the leaves at the top of the tree, and active transport in the plant.

Plant Reproduction

The majority of plants that reproduce via sexual reproduction are known as angiosperms. Angiosperms have flowers, which contain the reproductive organs. Flower parts include the sepals, petals, stamens, and carpels. The stamens and the carpels are not actual reproductive organs. The stamen holds the anther of the flower, which contains the pollen. The sepals are protective leaf-like structures at the base of the flower. Before the flower opens, the sepals can be seen as the greenish covering that envelops the flower bud. The carpels contain the ovaries of the plant, and each carpel has a long style that holds the ovary at the base. The ovaries are attached to a stigma that receives pollen during fertilization.

A "complete flower" is one that contains all of these basic flower organs. Many species of angiosperms do not contain complete flowers, including most grasses and some seed plants, such as sunflowers.

Gametophytes

Male Gametophytes – Pollen

The male gametophytes are known as pollen, and are housed inside the anther. Inside each anther there are structures called microsporangia. These structures contain the cells that undergo meiosis to produce pollen. After meiosis occurs, the cells form a spore wall and create a pollen grain.

Female Gametophytes – Embryo Sacs

The female gametophyte is best understood as an embryo sac. It is not a cellular "egg" as seen in most mammalian or animal reproductive systems.

Pollination

Pollination occurs when there is a transfer of pollen from the anther of one flower to the ovaries of another flower. Pollination can occur through many means, including wind, water, or animals/insects. Pollination by wind and insect are the most common types.

After pollination occurs, the following steps take place:

1. A pollen tube starts to grow down from the stigma to the ovaries.

2. The pollen tube, upon reaching the ovaries, will discharge two sperm cells into the embryo sac.

3. One sperm cell will be able to fertilize the egg, creating the zygote. The other sperm is involved in the formation of the endosperm, which grows into a nutritious layer that surrounds the zygote.

After fertilization, the endosperm starts developing. The endosperm stores nutrients that provide a buffer for the seedling after it germinates and sprouts. Examples of the endosperm include the grain of wheat, the white meat of a coconut and most fruits.

The embryo develops a little after the endosperm. After it has matured, the seed will have several parts: The epicotyl, the hypocotyl, the radicle, and the cotyledons. This seed structure is surrounded by the endosperm and then the seed coat.

Photosynthesis

Photosynthesis is the energy source for nearly all the biomass on Earth. The term is derived from "photo", meaning light, and "synthesis," meaning construction. Light energy is absorbed by plants and converted via photosynthesis into sugars. Organisms that are able to produce their own sustenance in this manner are known as autotrophs.

Chloroplasts

The chloroplasts are small organelles found in plant tissue that contain chlorophyll. Chlorophyll is a deep green compound, which is also responsible for most plants' green color. The chloroplasts are contained inside the mesophyll of the plant leaf – this is the section sandwiched between the top and bottom layers of the leaf.

Inside the chloroplast, there are two primary structures: The stroma, which is the envelope of the chloroplast, and the thylakoids, which are stacks of sacs that contain the chlorophyll.

The Chemistry of Photosynthesis

The overall chemical reaction of photosynthesis is as follows:

$$6\ CO_2 + 12\ H_2O + \text{Light energy} \rightarrow C_6H_{12}O_6\ (Glucose) + 6\ O_2 + 6\ H_2O$$

The photosynthesis reaction uses carbon dioxide and water, in addition to energy from sunlight, to produce glucose and oxygen. In this reaction, the carbon from carbon dioxide ends up in the glucose molecule. Half of the oxygen from carbon dioxide ends up in the glucose, and the other half ends up in the produced water. On the other hand, all of the oxygen from the water molecules on the reactant side of the equation ends up in the oxygen produced.

Oxygen production by photosynthesis is crucial to organisms that use aerobic respiration to get energy – including most animal life. In this way, plants and animals are symbiotic. Plants take in carbon dioxide produced by animal respiration and use it to make sugar and oxygen. The oxygen produced by plants is essential for continued animal respiration.

Similar to aerobic respiration, photosynthesis is an oxidation-reduction process, and relies on the transfer of electrons to be effective. These reactions take place in two phases. The first is in the light reactions, in which the energy from the sun is captured and translated into high-energy electrons. The second is in the Calvin cycle, where this energy is used in conjunction with carbon dioxide and water to produce a glucose molecule.

Light Reactions

The light reactions occur in the chloroplast. They take light from the sun, which is best absorbed by the chlorophyll between the wavelengths of 420 nm to 460 nm, and convert it into active electrons. The chlorophyll compound is a unique, massive, molecule especially capable of absorbing light energy. The image below portrays the structure of chlorophyll a:

The chlorophyll compound consists of a porphyrin ring, which absorbs photons. The absorption of the photon increases the energy level of an electron, elevating it to a higher energy orbital.

The acceptance of electrons in chlorophyll occurs in two systems: Photosystem I and Photosystem II. These systems work together to funnel high-energy electrons down to a terminal electron acceptor. The passage of electrons along the system is aided by molecules called quinones. At the end of the chain, the enzyme NADP+ reductase adds an electron to an NADP+ molecule, creating the energy storage molecule NADPH. The basic steps of the light reactions are as follows:

1. Light strikes PS II, energizing an electron.

2. The electron is transferred to a primary electron acceptor in P680, a compound in the chlorophyll.

3. An enzyme splits water, supplying two H+ ions and an oxygen atom. The H+ ions form a gradient across the lumen layer in the thylakoid membrane.

4. The energized electrons pass to PSI via a chain of quinone structures.

5. The transport of electrons helps to drive the gradient of H+ ions even further onto one side of the thylakoid membrane.

6. The enzyme NADP+ reductase takes the active electrons and catalyzes the formation of NADPH. Two electrons are needed for one molecule of NADPH.

The Calvin Cycle

Now that the energy molecules of NADPH have been produced by the light-fixing reactions, they can be used to fix carbon dioxide and turn it into glucose. The Calvin cycle is somewhat similar to the citric acid cycle, in that there is an intermediate compound (oxaloacetate in the TCA cycle) recycled after every round of synthesis. The Calvin cycle produces a sugar precursor, known as glyceraldehyde-3-phosphate (G3P):

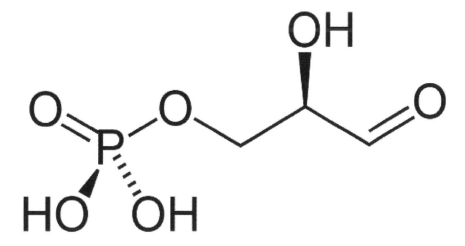

This is a 3-carbon molecule, and requires three cycles of the Calvin cycle, each time fixing one molecule of carbon dioxide. As a result, two molecules of G3P are required to create one 6-carbon glucose molecule.

The steps of the Calvin cycle are as follows:

1. Three CO_2 molecules are used by RuBisCo (Ribulose-1, 5-bisphosphate carboxylase/oxygenase), an enzyme, to produce six molecules of 3-phosphoglycerate.

2. 6-ATP is then used to convert the 3-phosphoglycerate into six molecules of 1, 3-bisphosphoglycerate, an activated compound.

3. 6-NADPH is then used to convert the 1, 3-bisphosphoglycerate into six molecules of glyceraldehyde-3-phosphate. At this point, one molecule of the G3P is exported for conversion to glucose or other materials, and five molecules of G3P continue in the cycle.

4. The five molecules of G3P, in addition to three ATP, are used to regenerate the three molecules of ribulose bisphosphate that catalyze the CO_2 fixation reaction.

Note that this is a very energy-intensive process. In order to make one G3P molecule, a plant has to expend nine units of ATP and six units of NADPH. These energy molecules are generated from light reactions that occur in the chloroplast.

C3 vs. C4 Plants

There are two types of carbon fixing plants in the world, and they are known as C3 and C4 plants, due to the number of carbons that the fixed molecule becomes. The majority of plants are C3, which fixes carbon into G3P.

C4 plants are rarer, and are seen in about 20 different plant families. Instead of fixing carbon into glycerylaldehyde-3-phosphate, these plants fix carbon into a 4-carbon molecule known as oxaloacetate, which becomes malate that is then transformed into pyruvate for the production of sugar or ATP.

The major difference between these plants is the manner in which they photorespirate. In order to get an adequate amount of carbon dioxide, plants need to have stomata open, which allows air to enter the leaf. This is typical in most C3 plants. However, in hot environments, such as the desert, having stomata open during the day, when the light fixing reactions take place, can be lethal. Thus, C4 plants use a different enzyme, called PEP carboxylase that can fix carbon dioxide even in very low concentrations. This eliminates the need to have stomata open during the day and reduces the amount of water lost due to photorespiration.

Important Facts to Remember about Photosynthesis

- Two sets of reactions occur. The light reactions generate ATP and NADPH, and the synthesis reactions use those molecules to create G3P.

- Plants need visible light between 400-460 nm wavelengths in order to generate high-energy electrons for the light reactions.

- The electron flow system in the plant chloroplast is quite similar to that of the mitochondria.

- There are two primary different types of carbon fixation: C3 and C4.

Fungi are heterotrophic organisms, meaning they feed off of biological matter produced primarily by plants. Most fungi use hydrolytic enzymes to digest wood or other types of biomass. These enzymes are able to dissolve the cell wall of plants, which is made of cellulose. The dissolved cellulose becomes glucose, which is a good food source.

Fungi have a unique diversity of structures, and can exist in a variety of forms from single-cell organisms, such as yeast, to larger mushrooms that have a distinctive shape. The body of the fungus has a system of root-like structures called hyphae. Hyphae are tubular cell structures that spread underground and function to penetrate into the fungi's food source. When you pull up a mushroom or notice some mold, the spidery-like film that may cover the root area is the hyphae.

Fungal Reproduction

Fungi can reproduce either sexually or asexually. In sexual reproduction, the fungi release chemical substances called pheromones that allow the spores from each fungi to identify each other. If the pheromones are compatible, then the two spores are able to fuse in a process called plasmogamy. This results in the creation of a dikaryotic joint nuclei.

Asexual reproduction is also quite common in fungi, with more than 20,000 species of fungi believed to be capable of reproducing asexually. In the asexual reproduction mechanism, the fungi will produce haploid spores through the process of mitosis. These spores are fully capable of developing into another fungi organism.

In addition, many single-celled fungi species, such as yeast and other molds, are able to reproduce asexually simply by dividing.

There are five major groups of fungi. They are:

1. *Chytrids* – These are single-celled or multi-celled globular fungi. The majority of fungi in this group are smaller than 100 μm.

2. *Zygomycetes* – This group is a type of mold and forms biofilms. They reproduce through production of spores.

3. *Glomeromycetes* – A small family of fungi very important for plant growth; many of them form symbiotic relationships with plants.

4. *Ascomycetes* – The largest group of fungi, these are known as sac fungi, and many of them are cup- or ear-shaped.

5. *Basidiomycetes* – These fungi contain many of the edible strains, and are the most typical "mushrooms".

Fungi in Ecology

Fungi are very important in the food chain and the surrounding ecology. They are very good at decomposing organic material, and are known for decomposing trees, leaves, and other plant biomass that fall to the forest floor. Some fungi also have the ability to degrade toxic chemicals, and can even be used to clean up oil spills. Finally, fungi work in a mutualistic fashion or symbiotically with many other species.

The union of a fungi and a cyanobacteria or algae is known as a lichen. Lichens are commonly found in moist environments, and can grow on rocks, trees, or other hard surfaces. The fungi help provide essential nutrients through the digestion of biomass, and the algae or cyanobacteria, which is photosynthetic, is able to provide a source of sugar to the fungi.

III

Cell Interactions

With the vast number of cells in living organisms, (an estimated 100 trillion in the human body), how do they all interact and talk with one another? Cells are able to communicate with one other through cell signaling, which occurs via chemical signals excreted by the cell. It is also possible to have direct cell-to-cell communication through protein receptors located in the cell membrane.

Local (Direct) Signaling

Local or direct signaling is a signal that occurs between cells that are either right next to each other, or within a few cells' distance. This can occur by two methods.

Firstly, gap junctions exist between the cell membrane of two cells that can allow signaling molecules to directly enter the cells. Secondly, the receptors on the cell membrane can bind with other cells that have membrane receptors to communicate.

Long Distance Signaling

The primary chemical used in long range signaling is called a hormone. In humans and animals, hormones are produced by organs and cells located in the endocrine system. Examples of organs in the endocrine system include the testes, hypothalamus, and pituitary glands. These hormones, once released, can travel throughout the organism through the circulatory pathway (blood). The hormones can then bind to other cells that have the appropriate receptor, and cause a signal to start inside the cell.

A good example of long range signaling in the human body is the production of insulin by the pancreas. Insulin spreads through the body via the blood circulation system, and when it binds to an insulin receptor on a cell, the cell begins to take in more glucose. This is long range signaling, because insulin is produced by cells in only one location (the pancreas) but is able to affect nearly all other cells in the body.

In plants, a good example of long range signaling is the production of ethylene, a ripening chemical. It can be present in the air, or diffuse through cell walls. The production of ethylene by one plant can cause a chain reaction that causes nearby plants to also start ripening.

Signal Transduction: The G-Protein Coupled Receptor

The G-protein coupled receptor (GPCR) is one of the most important types of signal transduction pathways, and will likely show up on the exam.

The GPCR is a large protein receptor that exists in the cell membrane. It is unique in that it uses energy in the form of GTP in order to start a signal cascade inside the cell. These types of receptors are found in nearly all types of eukaryotic cells, and consist of a structure of seven alpha-helix protein substructures, and a G-protein binding unit. A GPCR works in the following steps:

1. An activating signaling molecule will bind to the extra-membrane part of the GPCR. This causes GTP to attach to the GPCR and active the molecule.

2. The G-protein, activated by the GTP, dissociates from the membrane protein and binds to an activated enzyme. This enzyme can be either in the cell membrane (transport enzyme), or can be in the cell cytosol.

3. This bond causes the enzyme to activate, and can subsequently affect other pathways.

Important Signaling Molecules

- *Cyclic AMP* –an important molecule involved in signal cascades. It is best known for its function in the signaling cascade when epinephrine binds to a cell.

- *Common neurotransmitters* – these are molecules primarily used in the nervous system. They include glycine, aspartate, acetylcholine, and melatonin, among many others.

Programmed Cell Death: Apoptosis

Apoptosis is an elaborate cellular signaling mechanism that determines when a cell 'suicides', or dies. In normal animals and cells, apoptosis is a well-regulated occurrence that prevents the overgrowth of cells. In the process of apoptosis, enzymes and other cellular agents break down materials in the cell until the membrane dissociates and nothing remains.

Apoptosis has been observed in nearly all living organisms, and is an essential part of growth and regrowth. For example, in humans, our skin cells undergo apoptosis every day, with dead skin cells shedding off and new skin cells replacing them.

The mechanism of apoptosis is one of the most studied in biology due to its strong link with many cancers. Cancerous tumors can develop due to a failure of the apoptosis pathway, leading to the growth of cells that never die. (Note however, that cancer can be caused by many things, not just a lack of apoptosis).

There are two genes hypothesized to be the most important for apoptosis, known as the CED-3 and CED-4 genes. When activated, these genes start a signaling cascade that starts the production of *caspases*. Caspases are proteases (meaning they break down proteins). The presence of caspases starts the breakdown of proteins in the cell, resulting in a cell membrane filled with small bits of molecules that were formerly proteins or other organelles. The cell then starts to autolyse, with the cell membrane becoming porous, and eventually breaking apart.

Cell Division

Cell division is one of the most important processes a cell performs. It is used for reproduction and proliferation. Reproduction through mitosis is known as asexual reproduction, in that another partner cell is not required. Meiosis is sexual reproduction. Cell division is seen in nearly every single type of cells, from the development of muscle cells to the fertilization and beginning of an embryo.

Cell Mitosis

The Basics of Cell Division

When a cell divides, it needs to make sure that each copy of the cell has a roughly equal amount of the necessary elements, including DNA, proteins, and organelles.

A cell has quite a bit of DNA. Even the smallest human cell, for example, contains a copy of the entire human genome. A genome is the totality of the genetic information in a species. In human cells, this copy of the genome is nearly 2 meters in length – quite long when you consider that the average cell is only 100 μm in diameter.

The DNA is packaged tightly into units called chromatids, which are then further condensed into chromosomes. In prokaryotic organisms, which do not have a well-defined DNA structure, much of the DNA is present in plasmid form. Plasmids are circular rings of genetic information.

Before mitosis occurs, the cell needs to grow larger and accumulate additional copies of DNA and many of the organelles contained inside the cell. This is called the interphase, which takes about 80-90% of the total time of the cell cycle. During interphase, the cell is simply growing. After the cell reaches a certain point (determined by each individual cell), mitosis will begin, and the rest of the cycle begins.

The Cell Cycle

The cell cycle can be divided into 4 primary phases:

1. G1 phase – growth phase 1
2. S – phase – DNA replication

3. G2 phase – growth phase 2

4. Mitotic phase – The cell undergoes mitosis and splits.

The part that bears the most information is in the mitotic phase, which is separated into five substages:

- *Prophase* – In prophase, the DNA in the cell winds into chromatin and each pair of duplicated chromosomes become joined. The mitotic spindle, which pulls apart the chromosomes later, forms and drifts to each end of the cell.

- *Prometaphase* – In this phase, the nuclear membrane, which holds the DNA, dissolves, allowing the chromosomes to come free. The chromosomes now start to attach to microtubules linked to the centrioles.

- *Metaphase* - the centrioles, with microtubules attached to the chromosomes, are now on opposite sides of the cell. The chromosomes align in the middle of the cell, and the microtubules begin contracting.

- *Anaphase* – In anaphase, the chromosomes move to separate sides of the cell, and the cell structure begins to lengthen, pulling apart as it goes.

- *Telophase* – In this last part of the cell cycle, the cell membrane splits, and two new daughter cells are formed. The nucleolus, containing the DNA, reforms.

In this manner, cells are able to reproduce quite quickly. Many bacteria or yeast cells have a total cell cycle time of between 20-30 minutes, meaning they are able to double in number in that amount of time. This can lead to rapid proliferation of cells, assuming there is no food shortage. A small colony of 200 *E.coli* cells can rapidly grow to more than 20 million cells in a matter of hours.

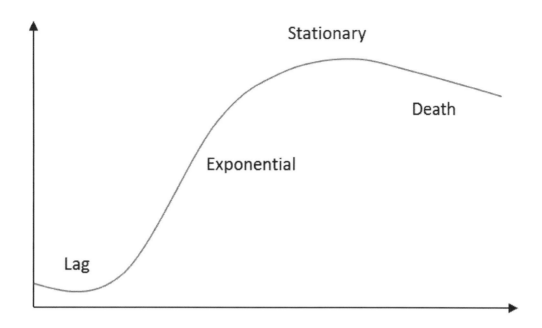

The diagram above shows how a colony of cells will typically act given a fixed amount of nutrients. After an initial lag phase in which the cells are growing, the cells will start to reproduce via mitosis, quickly growing higher and higher in number. As the nutrients start to be consumed, the cell growth will start to slow, eventually reaching stationary phase. If there are no nutrients, the death phase will begin, where cells die and are consumed by other cells. In the diagram, the X-axis represents time, and the Y-axis represents cell count.

Cell Meiosis

The steps in the meiotic process are roughly similar to those in mitosis, but with one important difference: the cells produced by meiosis are haploid, whereas those produced by mitosis are diploid. There are two consecutive stages of meiosis known as Meiosis I and Meiosis II, which result in four haploid daughter cells.

In the starting cell, there are pairs of homologous chromosomes. For example, recall that humans have 23 pairs of chromosomes, for 46 chromosomes total. After the end of Meiosis I, each daughter cell will have one chromosome each, or 26 each. After Meiosis II, there will be four daughter cells, each with a haploid version of the chromosome.

The full detailed process of Meiosis I and II are described on the next page.

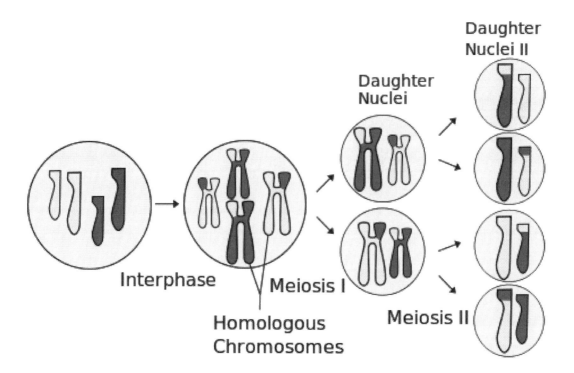

Meiosis I

1. *Prophase I* – In prophase, the chromosomes condense using histone proteins and become paired. The paired chromosomes will connect with each other via structures called the synaptonemal complexes. This is also known as synapsis. An important phase called crossing-over occurs at this point. Genetic material is exchanged between sister chromatids, resulting in a random assembly of homologous chromosomes. After this is complete, microtubules attach to the chromosomes and centrioles and begin to align them in the middle of the cell.

2. *Metaphase I* – Similar to mitosis, the chromosomes align in the middle of the cell and begin to pull apart from one another.

3. *Anaphase I* – The sister chromatids separate and move toward opposite sides of the cell.

4. *Telophase I* – The cells separate, and each cell now has one copy each of a homologous chromosomes.

Meiosis II

1. *Prophase II* – In prophase II, a spindle forms and aligns the chromosomes. No crossing-over occurs.

2. *Metaphase II* – In Metaphase II, the chromosomes again align at the metaphase plate. This time, however, when they are pulled apart, each daughter cell will not have the same copy of a sister chromatid. This is what results in genetic variance among offspring.

3. *Anaphase II* – As in Anaphase I, the sister chromatids pull apart to opposite ends of the cell.

4. *Telophase II* – The cell splits apart, resulting in four unique daughter cells.

Comparison between Mitosis and Meiosis

Event	Mitosis	Meiosis
DNA replication	Occurs in interphase	Occurs in interphase
# of Divisions	1	2
Synapsis?	Does not occur	Occurs in prophase I
Number of Daughter Cells	2	4
Role in Animals	Cell growth and repair	Production of gametes for reproduction

Introduction of Genetic Variation in Meiosis

Meiosis' most important utility is the introduction of genetic variation during crossing over. The independent assortment of chromosomes in this process gives each gamete a unique subset of genes from the parent. When the haploid gamete combines with another to form a zygote, the result is a genetically unique organism that has a different gene composition than either of the parents.

The sources of genetic variation are twofold:

• *Crossing Over* – In the crossing over process, recombinant genomes are produced. This occurs in prophase I, when the homologous chromosomes from the parent pair along their lengths. Each gene on each chromosome becomes aligned with its sister gene. Then, when crossing over occurs, the DNA sequence is broken and crisscrossed, creating a new chromatid with pieces of each of the original homologous chromosomes.

73

- *Random Fertilization* – The second source of genetic variation is in random fertilization. Although the gametes produced by each gender are unique, the fact that millions of sperm are produced by the human male (and quite a bit more in other species, such as plant pollen), means that there are many different possible combinations. For this reason, even though we might cross an animal pair together hundreds of times, it is next to impossible to get two children that have the same genotype (short of twins, of course).

The genetic variation produced by sexual reproduction plays a large role in evolution as well. Due to the wide range of possible phenotypic traits, variation means that a sexually reproducing organism has a good chance to introduce new phenotype traits that could be beneficial to surviving in an environment, rather than continually duplicating other traits.

Prior to Gregor Mendel's work in genetics, there were many conflicting theories on how offspring were conceived and why they were different. One of the dominant theories in the 19th century was the blending theory, the idea that genetic material from the parents would simply mix to form that of the children, in the same way that two colors might mix. However, according to this hypothesis, within a limited number of generations, the population would all look the same. After all, if each offspring were a perfectly blended combination of his or her two parents, then eventually, given enough random crossbreeding, everyone would be well blended together.

The idea that individual genes were passed down from father and mother to their children was conceived by Gregor Mendel. Mendel used various plants to found his ideas upon, and his best-known work is with pea plants.

Mendel's Pea Experiment

Mendel became an Augustinian monk at the age of 21. He studied briefly at the University of Vienna, and after returning to the monastery, Mendel started work on breeding plants. His work started with garden peas. During the course of his work, he discovered that there were heritable features, meaning features that were passed from parent to offspring, called characteristics, or traits. Because of the short generation time of peas, Mendel started working on identifying the traits that could be passed on in the pea plant. He tracked two characteristics: pea flower color and pea shape. From this, he found that traits are independent of one another, meaning that the pea's flower color in no way affected the pea shape.

Important Genetics Terms:

- *Homozygous* – A homozygous gene has two alleles of the same type.

- *Heterozygous* – A heterozygous gene has two different alleles.

- *Allele* – An allele is a part of a gene that may or may not be expressed.

- *P Generation* – Parent Generation

- *F Generation* – Filial Generation (F1, F2, F3 are all subsequent child generations)

Mendel's Laws

During the course of his work, Mendel came up with three laws to describe genetic inheritance:

1. *Law of Segregation* – This states that genes come in allele pairs (if the organism is diploid, which most are), and that each parent can only pass a single allele down to its child. Thus, for a pair of alleles in a gene, one comes from the father and one comes from the mother in sexual reproduction. The law of segregation also determined that during the course of meiosis, the alleles must separate, so that only one is given to each gamete.

2. *Law of Independent Assortment* – This states that genes responsible for different traits are passed on independently. This means that there is not necessarily a correlation between two genes. For example, if a mother is tall and has brown hair, she might pass on her genes for tallness to her child, but perhaps not the ones for brown hair. This law can be seen in the use of the Punnett square, in which gene alleles are separated to determine inheritance.

3. *Law of Dominance* – This states that some alleles are dominant and some are recessive. Dominant alleles will mask the behavior of the recessive alleles. A good example of dominance is rose color. Red is dominant, and white is recessive. Thus, if a homozygous red rose mates with a homozygous white rose, all of their offspring will be red. Although the white gene allele will be present, its behavior will be "dominated" by the red allele.

Punnett Square

A Punnett Square is a table-based diagram that can be used to predict the offspring outcome from the mating of a set of parents. It was developed by Reginald Punnett.

In the square, the alleles from each parent are placed on the X and Y axes of the square, and the boxes are then filled in to represent the possible offspring gene combinations. An example of how to perform a Punnett square is given below.

Example: Potatoes can be either round or oval. The dominant gene is oval. A heterozygous oval potato plant (Oo) is mated with a homozygous round potato plant (oo). The offspring can be predicted as:

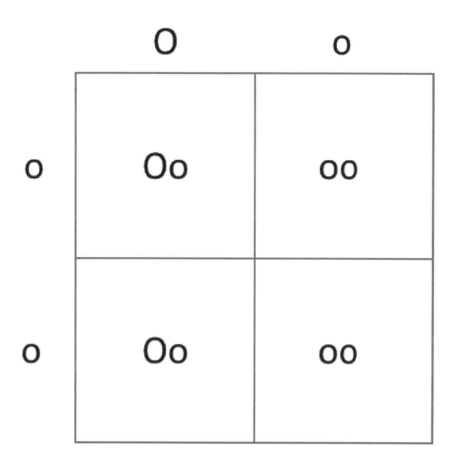

In the Punnett Square above, we have placed the parents on each side of the box. The heterozygous parent is seen on the X-axis as Oo, and the homozygous is on the Y-axis. By separating the alleles (the law of segregation) and then recombining the possible combinations from the parents, we can predict what the genotype, and thus phenotype, of the offspring will be. In this case, half of the offspring will be round (oo), and the other half will be oval (Oo).

A larger Punnett Square is useful to examine multiple gene allele sets. For example, we could look at potato flower color as well. Purple flowers are dominant, and pink flowers are recessive. If we had a OoPP parent crossed with a ooPp parent, what would the result look like?

	OP	OP	oP	oP
oP	OoPP	OoPP	ooPP	ooPP
oP	OoPP	OoPP	ooPP	ooPP
op	OoPp	OoPp	ooPp	ooPp
op	OoPp	OoPp	ooPp	ooPp

In this case, we separate out the alleles so that each one is matched with the other allele in all the possible combinations:

OoPP has four combinations: OP, OP, oP, and oP. This is each allele from the O gene matched with each allele from the P gene.

If we then use the same principle as for the smaller Punnett square, we can get a 4x4 square able to predict all the available offspring types.

Phenotype vs. Genotype

The scientific community is currently conducting a long-running conversation about phenotypes and genotypes. The phenotypes of an individual are the physical characteristics that they have. For example, height, eye color, skin color, and hair color are all examples of phenotypic traits. Genotype is the genetic information that lies behind the phenotype. Although the genotype of two different people might be different, they could have the same phenotype, depending on which alleles are dominant or recessive.

For example, the two types of roses Rr and RR are both red. They have the same phenotype. However, they have a different genotype, with one rose type being heterozygous and the other being homozygous.

The environment may have a large effect on the phenotypic traits. Environmental conditions such as nutrition, predators, or sunlight may change the phenotype of an individual. Even if someone has light brown skin, for example, if they spend enough time under the sun, their skin color will become a dark brown. Likewise, even though a person may be genetically inclined to be tall, if they do not receive enough nutrients or food in their youth, they may end up being short anyways.

DNA replication is the process by which a copy of DNA is created in an organism's genome. This process is necessary and is seen in all living organisms. Without DNA replication, mitosis or meiosis could not occur.

The Basics of DNA

Deoxyribonucleic acid, or DNA, is a unique structure that has two major parts: a nucleotide base and a sugar backbone. The DNA strand is a double helix structure consisting of two complementary strands of DNA. Each DNA strand has a deoxyribose sugar backbone, and the code consists of four nucleic acid bases: guanine, adenine, thymine, and cytosine. They are represented in DNA code by the letters *G*, *A*, *T*, and *C*.

Adenine and guanine are purine compounds, and thymine and cytosine are pyrimidine compounds. They are complementary to one another. A and T form a pair, and G and C form a pair. A cannot hydrogen bond with G, and C cannot bind with T.

The individual strands of DNA are directional, and the nomenclature for the direction in which the strand is flowing is determined by the ends of the DNA, known as the 3' end and the 5' end. In any given DNA sequence, the left hand side of the sequence is the 5' end and the right hand side is the 3' end, as seen below:

5'-ATGAATTGCCT-3'

If there are two complementary strands of DNA, one end starts at 5' and the other starts at 3', as seen below:

5'-ATGAATTGCCT-3'

3'-TACTTAACGGA-3'

This naming convention is needed to understand the direction of DNA replication, and where the enzymes bind during the process.

During DNA replication, three steps will occur:

1. *Initiation* - In this step, an initiator protein will bind to certain regions of DNA known as origin sites. Once the initiation protein has been bound, the DNA polymerase complex will be able to be able to attach. At this point, DNA will unwind into two separate single strands.

2. *Elongation* - During this step, new strands of DNA are created. Single strand binding proteins (SSBs) will bind to each strand of the DNA. Then, DNA polymerase will attach and start replicating the strands. DNA replication is always synthesized from the 5' to 3' direction, and DNA polymerase reads the DNA in the 3' to 5' direction. This creates a problem, because we can only read the DNA in the 3' to 5' direction on one strand. What happens to the other strand?

   - *Okasaki Fragments* – The other strand needs to be synthesized piece by piece, and the result is a length of DNA that has several 'chunks' of complementary sections, called Okasaki fragments. The breaks between these fragments are later filled in with DNA ligase.

3. *Termination* - After DNA polymerase completes the copying process, the replication forks meet and the process is terminated. There is one catch to this: because the DNA polymerase enzyme can never read or replicate the very end of a strand of DNA, every time a full chromosome is replicated, a small part of DNA is lost at the end. This piece of DNA is usually non-coding and is called a telomere. The shortening of the telomeres is the reason why replication can only occur a limited number of times in somatic cells before DNA replication is no longer possible.

Important Enzymes in DNA Replication

- *DNA Helicase* – Unwinds a section of DNA to create a segment with two single strands

- *DNA Polymerase* – DNA polymerase I is responsible for synthesizing Okasaki fragments. DNA polymerase III is responsible for the primary replication of the 5' to 3' strand.

- *DNA Ligase* – Ligase fixes small breaks in the DNA strand, and is used to seal the finished DNA strands.
- *DNA Telomerase* – In some cells, DNA telomerase lengthens the telomeres at the end of each strand of DNA, allowing it to be copied additional times.

Basics of Polymerase Chain Reaction (PCR)

PCR is a method used in biology to artificially replicate DNA. This can be useful to look at the presence or size of a gene, or in order to get enough DNA to put into a host organism. This process was developed in 1983. The PCR method uses primers, DNA polymerase, a template, and a machine called a thermo cycler in order to replicate the DNA. The basic steps are as follows:

1. *Denaturation* – The DNA is heated to 90+ °C to denature it and cause it to form single strands

2. *Annealing* – The reaction temperature is set to between 50-60 °C, which allows the primers to anneal to the template.

3. *Elongation* – The reaction temperature is set to 70-80 °C, which is an optimal temperature for a modified DNA polymerase called Taq polymerase. DNA replication occurs.

This set of steps is then repeated up to 100 times in the thermo cycler. As a result, if you start with 100 copies of DNA in the solution, after 40 cycles you will have 1.1×10^{14} copies of DNA.

DNA Transcription and Translation

DNA translation, also known as gene expression, is the path in the cell that takes the genetic information from a strand of DNA and transforms that information into a protein. There are two substages in this process: transcription and translation. In transcription, an mRNA copy of the DNA is created. In translation, the mRNA strand is read by a ribosome to create an amino acid chain, which is folded into a protein.

Transcription

DNA transcription is the process of making a copy of messenger RNA from a DNA strand. The two types of information are encoded in slightly different ways. DNA uses four bases: adenine, cytosine, guanine, and thymine, seen below:

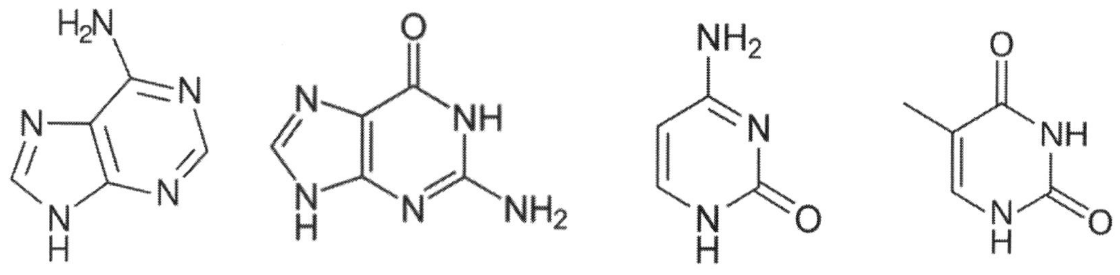

Adenine Guanine Cytosine Thymine

In RNA, the only difference is the replacement of the cytosine molecule with Uracil, seen below:

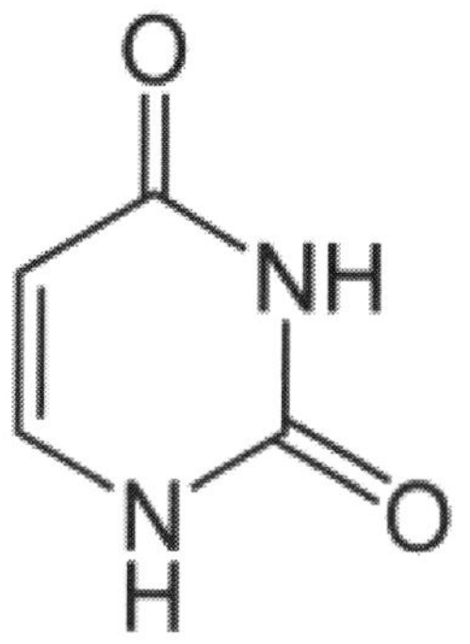

The DNA strand provides a template for RNA polymerase to work with. The steps for DNA transcription are similar to that of DNA replication, though using different enzymes. The DNA structure is first unwound, and then RNA polymerase makes a transcript of the DNA sequence.

After the primary transcript has been made, the mRNA is sent to spliceosomes, which remove the non-coding regions of the RNA represented by the introns. The final RNA product is then available for translation into the actual protein.

Codons

The "message" contained in DNA and RNA is encoded in a triplet code. Each amino acid is represented by a set of three base pairs in the sequence. This allows there to be 64 different codon combinations (4 x 4 x 4 combinations). The instructions for the amino acid sequence are read by a protein complex called a ribosome, which then assembles the amino acid.

The codon table is seen below:

1st base	2nd base				3rd base
	U	C	A	G	
U	UUU (Phe/F) Phenylalanine	UCU (Ser/S) Serine	UAU (Tyr/Y) Tyrosine	UGU (Cys/C) Cysteine	U
	UUC	UCC	UAC	UGC	C
	UUA (Leu/L) Leucine	UCA	UAA Stop (Ochre)	UGA Stop (Opal)	A
	UUG	UCG	UAG Stop (Amber)	UGG (Trp/W) Tryptophan	G
C	CUU (Leu/L) Leucine	CCU (Pro/P) Proline	CAU (His/H) Histidine	CGU (Arg/R) Arginine	U
	CUC	CCC	CAC	CGC	C
	CUA	CCA	CAA (Gln/Q) Glutamine	CGA	A
	CUG	CCG	CAG	CGG	G
A	AUU (Ile/I) Isoleucine	ACU (Thr/T) Threonine	AAU (Asn/N) Asparagine	AGU (Ser/S) Serine	U
	AUC	ACC	AAC	AGC	C
	AUA	ACA	AAA (Lys/K) Lysine	AGA (Arg/R) Arginine	A
	AUG[A] (Met/M) Methionine	ACG	AAG	AGG	G
G	GUU (Val/V) Valine	GCU (Ala/A) Alanine	GAU (Asp/D) Aspartic acid	GGU (Gly/G) Glycine	U
	GUC	GCC	GAC	GGC	C
	GUA	GCA	GAA (Glu/E) Glutamic acid	GGA	A
	GUG	GCG	GAG	GGG	G

Each amino acid is represented by more than one codon sequence. There are 22 major amino acids represented. In addition there is something called a "stop" codon, which instructs the ribosome to stop processing the mRNA.

During the translation process, the codons are read in the 5' → 3' direction. Each codon is three base pairs, and thus a sequence of 600 base pairs in an mRNA strand would result in a 200-amino acid protein.

Ribosomal Translation

The translation process converts the mRNA transcript into a useable protein. In this process, there are several players. They are the tRNA (transport RNA) molecules, the amino acids, the mRNA transcript and the ribosome.

Each tRNA is a unique protein able to recognize a particular codon. Each tRNA molecule is also bonded to an amino acid. Thus, the tRNA will interact with the mRNA and the ribosome to correctly place the amino acid in order according to the information on the mRNA. After the tRNA molecule places the amino acid in the ribosome, a reaction occurs. The reaction is catalyzed by aminoacyl-tRNA synthetase. This enzyme uses a molecule of ATP to form an amino acid bond between the existing amino acid strand and the new amino acid been brought in by the tRNA.

The translation process stops when a stop codon is reached in the sequence. The three possible stop codons are UAG, UAA, and UGA. They do not code for amino acids. Instead, they are able to recognize a protein called a release factor, which binds to the ribosome. The ribosome, which is made of two units of protein, will split apart after the release factor binds. This releases the newly formed amino acid chain.

Protein Folding

After the amino acid chain has been produced, the process is still not complete. The amino acid chain needs to be folded into a protein. The polypeptide chain, now able to interact with itself due to hydrogen and disulfide bonds, will start to form into a three-dimensional structure. A protein has four primary levels of structure:

1. *Primary structure* – This structure is simply the amino acid sequence itself

2. *Secondary structure* – These structures such as alpha helixes and beta sheets. They are interactions within the amino acids, but do not form a whole 3-D structure.

3. *Tertiary structure* – The tertiary structure is the structure of a protein as a whole.

4. *Quaternary structure* – This structure is the interaction of a protein with more than one other protein. Examples include hemoglobin and some chelated metal-protein complexes.

Mutations

The DNA or RNA sequence can sometimes undergo a mutation, which is a change in the base pair sequence of the DNA or RNA strand. A mutation can be benign or silent, meaning it has no effect, or it can cause a change in the protein structure. An example of how a single point mutation can change the entire tertiary structure of a protein is sickle-cell anemia.

In sickle cell anemia, there is a single change in the base pair sequence from T to A. This results in an mRNA transcript codon change from GAA to GUA, which changes the amino acid from glutamate to valine. As a result, the protein is unable to fold properly, and the hemoglobin structure is longer than usual.

When present in a red blood cell, this mutation causes the red blood cells to become elongated and 'sickle-like'. As a result, oxygen is not carried as effectively in individuals who have sickle cell anemia.

On the other hand, many mutations will not result in any change in the protein sequence at all. For example, if the sequence CCG mutated to CCA, there would be no change, because the codon produced by both sequences will represent the amino acid glycine.

Gene regulation is an important part of life. Although we know now how genes produce proteins and other structures, a very important part of understanding metabolism is learning how genes are activated, deactivated and changed.

Learning about gene expression and regulation is easier by studying bacteria, due to their simple genomes and the simplicity of extracting their plasmids. Although human gene regulation is becoming more thoroughly understood, the vast complexity of the human metabolism and number of genes makes it difficult to get a full picture of all the interactions.

There are two general ways of managing enzyme use in a bacteria: through managing the enzyme itself, through substrates or inhibition, and through the regulation of a gene.

In bacteria, one of the primary units involved in gene regulation is called an operator. An operator is a "switch" of DNA that helps enzymes locate that segment of DNA and understand when to start transcribing it. The location of the operator can be inside the promoter region of DNA or it can be between the promoter region and the coding region of the DNA.

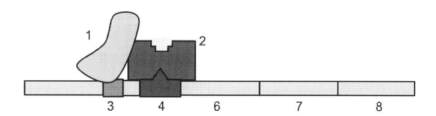

In the figure above, which represents a typical gene sequence, the numbers represent:

1. *RNA polymerase* – responsible for transcribing the region of DNA

2. *Repressor protein* – if attached, it prevents transcription of the DNA

3. *Promoter region* – this region 'attracts' the RNA polymerase to bind to the DNA

4. *Operator* – This region 'operates' the gene. If the switch is on, then the repressor falls off. If the switch is off, then the repressor remains in place and the gene cannot be transcribed.

93

5. Regions 6-8 are regions of coding DNA

Either negative or positive feedback is used to control the operon.

In a negative feedback operon, a repressor protein is bound to the operator in the normal state. Thus, in the normal state, the gene cannot be accessed. If an inductor molecule attaches, such as lactose, glucose, or some other substrate, the repressor protein falls off and transcription can begin.

In positive feedback operons, the gene is always on until there is overproduction of a substrate in the cytosol. At this point, the substrate will bind to the repressor protein, which allows it to come off, enabling the gene sequence to be transcribed.

Chromatin Regulation

Genes can also be regulated by managing how tightly bound the chromatin is in the nucleus. The location of the promoters in the chromatin sequence greatly affects the access of the gene. The modifications to the chromatin can change which genes can be expressed. The modifications include histone modifications, DNA methylation, and epigenetics.

Histone Modification

Histone proteins are small amino acid structures that can help to wind DNA. There is scientific evidence that shows histone proteins are affected by their bond to a lysine unit. When the lysine unit on a histone tail is acetylated, the histone tail cannot bind to nearby DNA, and allows the DNA to become unwound. When the tail becomes acetylated, the histone protein is able to rewind the DNA.

DNA Methylation

DNA can be methylated at the cytosine group. The methylation of DNA will prevent a DNA polymerase or RNA polymerase enzyme from attaching to the DNA, in effect preventing transcription.

IV

Evolution

Evolution is best defined as descent from previous species with modification. That is, each generation changed slightly from the last. Evolution is why there is a diversity of life on Earth – the reason there are different *species* of animals and plants. This was what Charles Darwin meant by the title of his book *The Origin of Species*.

Charles Darwin

Charles Darwin was an Englishman with an intense interest in nature. Darwin enrolled at several universities, including Cambridge. He became interested in botany there, and had a chance to accompany the HMS Beagle on a voyage around the world. It was during this trip that he came across numerous species, and was able to start forming the theory of evolution.

The HMS Beagle traveled to many locations, including large parts of the South American coastline. During this time, Darwin was able to observe many species and collect samples. However, the most productive stop of the HMS Beagle was at an island group called the Galapagos. There, Darwin found an unusual array of species, as well as many bird species that seemed similar to one other, but had some distinguishing characteristics. Here, Darwin came up with the idea that different birds developed various adaptations in order to survive in a unique environment.

Upon his return, Darwin published a book called *The Origin of Species*. It is worth noting that Darwin did not coin the term evolution at this time, but rather called it "descent with modification". He stated that all organisms were inter-related, and could be traced to a distant ancestor a long time ago. He was also one of the first to describe evolution as a tree, with different species branching off at different parts of the "tree".

Based on his observations, Darwin proposed a theory of Natural Selection.

Natural Selection

Charles Darwin noticed that there were some strong coincidences in his observations of birds on the island. Although many of the birds had a similar body shape, the birds had uniquely shaped beaks. Some beaks were small, some were wide and blunt, and some were needle like. Darwin hypothesized that these different beak shapes arose due to a selection process.

A selection process, whether natural or artificial, refers to the removal of inferior organisms that cannot survive in an environment. For example, farmers use artificial selection on their fields all the time. Farmers always want the crops that can produce the most yield, or the largest fruit. As a result, the fruits that we eat today are more three to four times larger than fruit that existed hundreds of years ago.

Darwin proposed the theory of natural selections based on specific observations. These were:

1. The members of a population of species have varied traits. For example, one species of monkey might have fur color varying from white to brown.

2. All species produce excess offspring. For example, if left uncontrolled, rabbit populations will more than double in size every year. Secondly, not all offspring are able to survive.

3. The traits in an individual of a population that give it a higher chance of surviving also allow it to produce more offspring.

4. As a result, "more fit" individuals are more likely to pass on their traits; this will result in a change in the species over time.

This is the basis of natural selection. Essentially, the traits of an individual determine whether it is "selected" by the environment. Individuals with superior traits are more likely to survive and reproduce, and thus pass on their genes. Individuals with inferior traits will not survive, and their genes will be lost. Over many generations, natural selection will lead to a species being driven toward a certain set of characteristics, and this is how evolution occurs.

Case Study: Drug-Resistant Bacteria

Antibiotics and other chemicals are commonly used to treat infections. This has, over the course of the last 20-30 years, created a selection of bacteria.

Staphylococcus aureus is a dangerous bacteria that resides on the skin of many people. It is ordinarily harmless, but if the individual has a weakened immune system, or the bacteria are allowed to enter the body in large amounts, *S. aureus* will eat away at the flesh of that person. This is the reason it is called the flesh-eating disease, or necrotizing fasciitis.

The best drug to treat *S. aureus* infections is methicillin, which was developed in 1959. However, just several years after the use of methicillin was introduced, methicillin-resistant *S. aureus* bacteria began to appear, nicknamed MRSA. How did this happen?

The use of antibiotics will usually kill 99.9% of the bacteria, but some bacteria will manage to survive, through either genetic resistance or an insufficient dose. These bacteria have been artificially selected. Over time, as more and more people use the antibiotic, the chance for a resistant strain of bacteria due to mutation will increase. This eventually results in the creation of a new trait in the *S. aureus* - methicillin resistance.

Today, more than half of *S. aureus* infections are methicillin-resistant, causing doctors to have to look elsewhere for an effective method of treatment. This is a present-day study of evolution in progress. Fifty years ago, there were no methicillin-resistant bacteria. However, due to continued exposure, and the fact that some bacteria manage to survive each time, the selection pressure has resulted in short-term evolution.

Interestingly, both sexual and asexual reproduction occurs in the animal kingdom, but the predominant form of reproduction is sexual, involving a sperm and an egg. Some examples of asexual reproduction in animals are the rotifer or the whiptail lizard, in which the female of the species is able to reproduce asexually.

The Sexual Cycle

Sexual reproduction in animals occurs in cycles, dependent on the production of an ovule, or egg, by the female of the species. In humans, the reproductive cycle occurs approximately once a month, when an egg is released from the females ovaries.

The female reproductive organs, or gonads, are called ovaries. Each ovary has a follicle that contains oocytes, or undeveloped eggs. The surrounding cells in the ovary help to protect and nourish the oocyte until it is needed. During the menstrual cycle, one oocyte will mature into an egg, and will be released into the fallopian tube, where it makes its way to the uterus.

Important terminology for the female reproductive system:

- *Corpus luteum* – a mass of follicular tissue that accompanies the egg and provides nutrients. It secretes estradiol and progesterone.

- *Uterus* – The location where the egg implants after being fertilized. The lining of the uterus is called the endometrium.

- *Cervix* – The opening from the uterus into the vagina.

- *Mammary Glands* – organs that produce milk in mammals to feed offspring.

Important terminology for the male reproductive system:

- *Leydig Cells* – These cells, which are in the scrotum, produce testosterone and other hormones.

- *Testes* – The testes are the male reproductive organs and produce sperm.

- *Vas deferens* – A muscular duct through which the sperm and semen flow.

- *Prostate* – A gland that produces nutrients and enzymes that accompany the sperm.

Embryo Fertilization and Development

Fertilization occurs when a sperm meets with the egg. After fertilization has occurred, the cell will start to divide about 24 hours later, and will become a ball of cells known as a blastocyst after four to five days. The blastocyst is then implanted into the endometrium of the uterus. At this point, the female body will start producing human chorionic gonadotropin, or hCG. hCG is the chemical detected in pregnancy tests. Thus, pregnancy tests will only show a positive result about five days or more after the actual act of fertilization has occurred.

After the blastocyst has been implanted onto the endometrium, the placenta develops. The placenta is a temporary organ that attaches the embryo to the mother. It provides nutrients derived from the mother's body. The placenta develops from cells called the trophoblast, which come from the outer layer of the blastocyst.

In humans, the gestation, or carrying period of the embryo, is 266 days or roughly 8.8 months. The gestation period varies widely among mammals. Rodents such as mice have gestation periods as short as 3 weeks, whereas elephants have a gestation period of over a year.

Human Development in the Womb

The human development cycle in the womb is divided roughly into three trimesters:

1. In the first trimester, the organs responsible for the embryo's growth develop. This includes the placenta and umbilical cord. During this time, organogenesis occurs, and the various stem cells from the blastocyst differentiate into the organs of the body. The organs are not fully developed at this point, but they exist.

2. In the second trimester, the fetus experiences rapid growth, up to about 25-30 cm in length. At this point, it is apparent that the woman is pregnant, as the uterus grows and extends, and the woman's belly becomes slightly distended.

3. In the third trimester, the fetus finishes developing. In humans, the average birth weight is3-4 kg, or 6.2 to 8.1 lbs.

Phylogeny is the understanding of how species evolved through time. The study of phylogeny creates charts called phylogeny trees, which show the inter-relatedness of different species. For example, humans are quite closely related to many mammals, with our DNA being 90% similar to that of cats.

The Phylogenetic Tree

A phylogenetic tree, shown in the diagram below, shows how groups of organisms are related to each other. The branches represent the relative point in time when each group of species, or family, diversified. For example, we can say according to the tree below that animals and fungi are more closely related than animals and flagellates, due to the distance comparison on the tree.

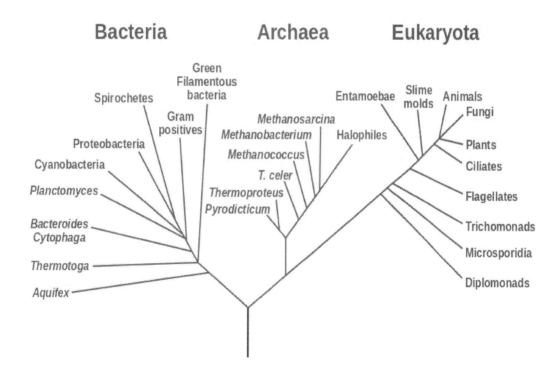

This type of diagram is useful for showing relationships in genetics, but not necessarily actual physical similarity. It should be easy to see that although animals and fungi might share a lot of DNA, they definitely have almost no similar phenotypic characteristics.

The diagram is also relative in nature, meaning that no absolute geologic time scale can be assigned to the branches. We know from the fossil record and DNA evidence which species are more closely related than others are; this allows us to construct the tree. However, other than a rough estimation on when the branches actually occurred, we cannot put exact numbers on the ages of the species.

Species Classification – Taxonomy

Taxonomy is the science of grouping species into correct taxa, or related groups. Groups descend in nature of similarity. For example, the 'kingdom' group is less similar than the 'genus' group. The current classification of species follows this order:

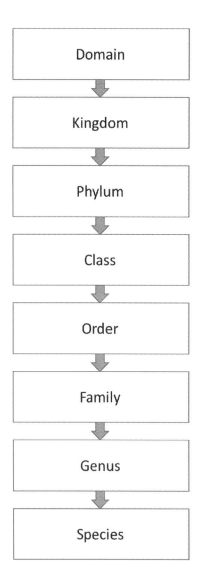

According to this organization, two species from the same phylum are more related than two species from the same order. A good mnemonic to remember this organization scheme is: *King Phillip Cried Out For Good Soup!*

The first letter of each word is related to the first letter of each name in the species classification.

Morphological Similarities Between Species

In closely related species, there are many phenotypic similarities. One of the most common similarities is in bone structure. Many animals from the same family share similar morphologies. This is due to a very close similarity in DNA sequences. For example, most primates have about a 99% DNA similarity, meaning that from chimpanzee to gorilla to human, the DNA sequence is 99% similar.

There is a distinction however, between a homologous structure and an analogous one:

- *Homologous*: A homologous structure is a phenotype structure that is similar due to genetic relatedness, as in one species evolved from another, or two species both evolved from a common ancestor. A good example of a homologous structure is the thumb. In the fossil record and from present day analysis, the thumb bone is seen in nearly all mammalian species. This is because they were all derived from a common ancestor.

- *Analogous*: An analogous structure is one not based on DNA similarity or shared ancestry. A good example of an analogous structure is the comparison between a bird wing and a bat wing. Upon looking at the bone structure, there are some similarities, but the two species have a completely different genetic history. As a result, it would be incorrect to conclude that birds and bats are closely related.

Life on Earth is proposed to have started about 3.5 billion years ago. The exact time when the first living cells appeared is unknown, but observations in geology have indicated the type of environment when living cells first appeared. It is hypothesized that life began due to the appearance of several types of molecules:

1. Synthesis of amino acid molecules and sugars, possibly from interaction of lightning and high temperatures near volcanic vents.

2. Joining and interaction of these molecules in something resembling modern-day proteins.

3. Assembly of these molecules within a membrane, which started to resemble a cell.

The researchers Stanley Miller and Harold Urey had a hypothesis that the above three steps could have happened in a primordial environment in which there was no oxygen. Note that higher concentrations of oxygen did not appear until the evolution of plants, so life must have started without a significant oxygen presence.

Miller-Urey Experiment

In the Miller-Urey experiment, the researchers placed a mixture of ingredients that included water, methane, ammonia, and hydrogen into an enclosed reactor bulb. The conditions were then simulated to those that were thought to exist on Earth several billion years ago. A pair of electrodes was placed into the reactor vessel, and sparks that simulated lightning were fired through the mixture every few minutes.

As a result, Miller and Urey found that their reaction mixture turned pink in color within a day, and after two weeks, the reactor vessel contained a thick solution that had an interesting number of ingredients.

Among the compounds that formed included some amino acids, including glycine, as well as sugars. After full characterization, the scientists found that the experiment created 11 of the 22 known amino acids.

Fossil Record

The fossil record is a history of species that existed throughout time, unearthed by archaeologists. The fossils, if well preserved, are able to show us the bone structures and the forms of animals, plants, and even cells that existed billions of years ago. The fossils can be used to understand how species evolved through time, and in some cases, even to see what they ate, and the environments in which they lived.

Fossils are dated through a method called radiometric dating, which examines the amount of radioactive carbon remaining in the sample. The radioactive carbon isotope, carbon-14, has a half-life of 5,730 years. This means that we can use this isotope to reliably date fossils that are up to about 10 half-lives, or 50,000 years in age. For fossils older than that, we need to use an isotope that has an even longer half-life. In some fossils, the presence of small amounts of uranium-238 can aid in dating with a half-life of 4.5 billion years.

Timeline of Earth

- 4.6 billion years ago – Formation of Earth

- 3.7 billion years ago – Prokaryotes first came into existence

- 2.6 billion years ago – Oxygen is believed to be present in the atmosphere

- 2.1 billion years ago – Eukaryotic organisms have evolved

- 1.5 billion years ago – Multicellular organisms have evolved

- 800 million years ago – The first animals exist

- 500 million years ago – Paleozoic Era

- 260 million years ago – Mesozoic Era

- 100 million years ago – Cenozoic Era

- 10,000 years ago – Early Humans

Characteristics of the "Life" Eras

The three eras, the Paleozoic, Mesozoic, and Cenozoic, were characterized by an explosion of different species. Each era was responsible for the formation of a number of different species.

- *Paleozoic* – The Paleozoic era was characterized by the colonization of land, with many types of plants appearing, and the diversification of fish and reptile species.

- *Mesozoic* – The Mesozoic era saw the first flowing plants appearing, as well as many land animals, including the dinosaurs. However, at the end of the Mesozoic era, the extinction of the dinosaurs occurred, likely due to a catastrophic event such as a huge meteorite striking the earth.

- *Cenozoic* – In the Cenozoic era, many of the animals and plants that we see today started to evolve, including mammals, many different angiosperm plants, and the direct ancestors of humans.

V

The Immune System

The immune system is used to detect pathogens and remove or prevent them from causing damage to an organism. These immune system cells include cells such as macrophages, which can engulf invading pathogens, to T-cells, which use antibodies to help other immune cells recognize pathogens. The immune system in the human body is based on the production of white blood cells, which serve many different purposes.

Layers of Defense

Two categories of immune defense help prevent sickness. The first is called barrier defense, which consists of physical barriers that prevent pathogens from entering the body. They include:

- Skin

- Mucous membranes

- Secretions

In humans, the skin is a remarkable layer of defense. The skin has between six and nine layers of skin cells that do an excellent job of preventing the entry of microbes or toxins. In fact, the majority of human disease comes from entry through the mucous membranes, in the mouth, eyes, or nose.

Internal defenses are located inside the body and help to eliminate a pathogen after it has gotten past the physical defenses. They include:

- Phagocytic cells

- Natural killer cells

- Antimicrobial proteins

- Histamine and inflammatory responses

These defenses work in concert to identify a foreign antigen or pathogen and eliminate it.

In mammals, the immune system cells are composed of two main types: neutrophils and macrophages. Neutrophils will recognize a pathogen signal and go to the site of infection to attack and absorb pathogens. Macrophages can be thought of as waste disposal cells. They reside in a central location, such as the spleen, and absorb and digest dead cells or pathogens. Remember that many cells die naturally in the human body, and the body needs a way to get rid of these.

Pathogen Recognition System

When a pathogen enters the human body, lymphocytes are the cells that recognize it. Lymphocytes are categorized into B cells and T cells. B and T cells have receptors in the cell membrane that are able to recognize antigens as "not-self." Essentially, they are programmed to be able to understand which molecules come from the human body and which cells are not. The programming comes from the major histocompatibility complex, or MHC, which determines an immune response.

Sometimes, the MHC will register a false positive – recognizing an antigen when there isn't one present at all. This is the cause of allergic reactions and autoimmune diseases. For example, although peanut butter is not harmful to the human body, those who are allergic have an immune system that recognizes it as a deadly antigen. The immune system springs into action, causing swelling from histamines and the over-production of white blood cells in an attempt to protect the body from this "invader." This is an allergic reaction and in severe cases, can cause death.

When a pathogen enters the body, the following steps take place, as illustrated by the diagram on the next page:

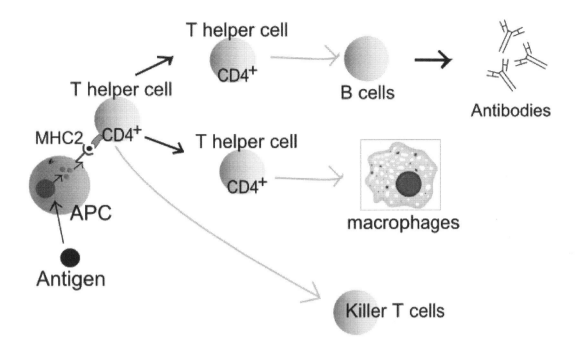

1. An antigen invades the body. For example, we will use a virus. The antigen infects a cell, which becomes the antigen-presenting cell (APC). This causes the proteins expressed on the cell's surface to change.

2. The changed proteins and the antigen are recognized by a T-helper cell that, when activated, produces a chemical called a cytokine. This promotes the activity of other cells, such as macrophages and Killer T cells.

3. The third step involves the activation of multiple different types of white blood cells:

   - *B cells*: B cells use antibodies to recognize and attack the antigen. The antibodies will be able to attach to the surface to the antigen, which then marks them for destruction by other phagocytes or macrophages.

   - *Killer T cells*: The killer T cells travel to infected cells and release cytotoxins that dissociate and destroy cell membranes.

   - *Macrophages*: Macrophages, when activated by helper T cells, detect invading antigens and engulf them through phagocytosis. Once engulfed, lysozymes are used to destroy the antigen.

Inflammatory Response

One of the immune responses is the use of histamine release at a wound site. The release of histamine causes swelling and an increase of body temperature at the site. Histamine causes blood vessels nearby the injury site to dilate, becoming larger and allowing more white blood cells to access the area. The white blood cells excrete cytokines to help eliminate the antigen. However, cytokines can also be damaging to tissue cells that are not dangerous. This causes the pain and swelling at an injury site that has become infected, such as a small cut.

Bacteria and Archaea are a large subset of species that are mostly unicellular. Unlike the kingdoms Plantae and Animalia, nearly all of these species are single-celled prokaryotes.

Prokaryotes are unicellular organisms that are quite small, usually less than 10 μm in diameter. In comparison, the smallest eukaryotic cells are usually larger than 10μm.

Like plants, prokaryotes have a cell wall. However, unlike plants, the cell wall structural material is called peptidoglycan, which is a polymer created by a mixture of cross-linked proteins and sugar. The cell wall supporting material in plants is called cellulose, which is made entirely from glucose, a sugar.

The presence of the cell wall allows prokaryotes to be separated into two classes: gram-positive and gram-negative.

This is how Archaea cells can be distinguished from bacteria. Archaea cell walls contain a cross-linked polysaccharide, but do not have any peptidoglycan. As a result, they are gram-negative.

Gram-positive bacteria contain peptidoglycan in their cell walls, and they turn purple-red when dyed with gram stain (a solution of crystal violet and iodine.)

DNA in Bacteria and Archaea

As prokaryotes, none of the bacteria or Archaea species contain nuclear membranes. All of the DNA is freely arranged within the cytosol in a structure called the nucleoid. In addition to the chromosomal DNA contained inside the nucleoid, the cells also contain plasmids, which are ring-shaped DNA sequences that contain an active gene. On the next page, you will find a sample plasmid called pCML15:

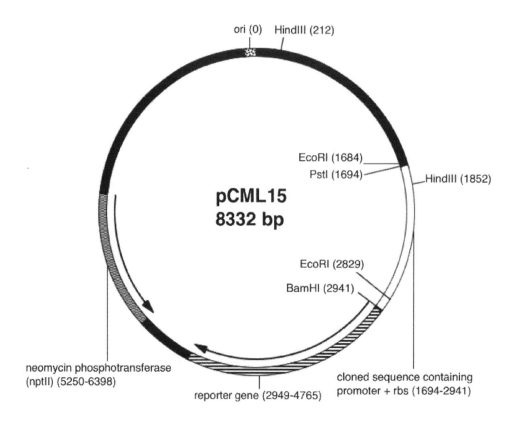

The bacterial plasmids used in research contain four major regions: the reporter gene, a restriction sequence, the expressed gene, and the origin site.

- *Reporter gene*: The reporter gene is a sequence that either expresses some colored compound or has antibiotic resistance. If the plasmid is resistant to penicillin, for instance, the reporter gene will contain that information.

- *Expressed gene*: The expressed gene is the gene that codes for some protein, such as laccase, glucose oxidase or another enzyme.

- *Restriction site*: The restriction site on a plasmid is a particular sequence of DNA that a restriction enzyme will be able to cut. Restriction enzymes are specific to a sequence, and are able to cut DNA exactly at that location.

- *Origin*: This is the origin site of the plasmid, or the "zero point."

A virus is a special form of organism designed to be infectious. Its name is derived from the Latin word for poison. Viruses are interesting organisms that do not contain organelles or other structures usually found in living creatures. For this reason, the question of whether viruses are alive or not has been a subject of serious debate.

What is the Definition of Life?

Scientists debate many different definitions of life, but in general, there is agreement on the following characteristics:

1. *Growth*: A living organism must be able to grow, usually by converting some external material into its own mass.

2. *Stimulus Response*: A living organism must be able to react to stimuli in its environment, such as light, other organisms, or toxins.

3. *Metabolism/Energy use*: A living organism must be able to use energy and convert energy into different forms, either as heat or as a stored energy compound.

4. *Homeostasis*: A living organism must be able to maintain its own organism conditions within a certain level. Examples might be sugar concentration in a cell, or body temperature for animals.

5. *Reproduction*: Living organisms must be able to reproduce.

6. *Mutation*: The genetic code of living organisms must be able to change between generations

7. *Autonomous motion*: Living organisms must be able to move, even if it is just a short distance (most cells can move).

Under these requirements, the majority of scientists do not consider viruses to be alive. This is because they do not have a metabolism of their own, and cannot reproduce by themselves. They require a host.

Virus Structure

A virus' structure is simple: it consists of a protein coat, known as a capsid, which surrounds a nucleic acid, which is either DNA or RNA. The capsid is a tough layer of protein that is resistant to heat, moisture, and other environmental variables. It protects the genetic information inside the virus, and usually has some sort of receptor or protein on the capsid that allows the virus to inject its DNA to a host organism.

Virus Reproduction

Viruses inject their DNA or RNA into other organisms in order to reproduce. They are obligate parasites in this manner. An obligate parasite is "obligated" to infect something in order to survive. In most cases, a virus will enter a host, and through an interaction of the proteins on the capsid, will be able to infect a host cell, use the host cell's energy and resources to reproduce, and then lyse the host cell, creating more virus cells. This is known as the lytic cycle. The lytic cycle of a typical virus, called a bacteriophage, is detailed below:

1. *Attachment*: the virus bonds to the host cell using proteins on the capsid.

2. *Entry*: The proteins inject DNA into the host cell

3. *Synthesis & reproduction*: the DNA is replicated using the host cell's 'machinery'.

4. *Assembly*: New viruses are assembled from the reproduced parts in the cell.

5. *Lysis & Release*: The virus destroys the host cell, lysing the cell membrane and releasing the newly created virus cells.

RNA Viruses

Some viruses contain RNA genomes rather than DNA. Among these viruses is the human immunodeficiency virus, or HIV. These viruses inject RNA, and the RNA can be translated into proteins or enzymes directly after infection.

In order for this method of transmission to work, the virus must carry some RNA reverse transcriptase. This protein is able to translate RNA back into DNA, so that the host organism can utilize it. Most RNA viruses are extremely dangerous, due to the human body's inability to effectively recognize it, since it uses RNA rather than DNA to attack.

Virus Evolution

Although viruses are not "alive" per se, they are capable of evolving very quickly due to their short life cycle and their ability to use a host genome. Many viruses are capable of assimilating other pieces of DNA into their own genome, often creating a new virus. Recently, the world has had to confront two new, frightening illnesses: Avian flu and swine flu. If these viruses interacted with human strains of influenza, they could assimilate parts of that genome into themselves, allowing them to infect humans. If such an evolutionary event were to occur, the added toxicity from the parts of the genome from the swine flu and avian flu, now added into the human influenza virus, could be problematic and dangerous.

VI

Ecology

Ecology is a broad aspect of biology and includes several levels of study. Common ecological questions include:

- How do humans affect the environment?

- How do species change or shift if environmental factors change?

- How do species interact with one another in an environment?

To answer these questions, there are categorized levels of ecological study:

1. *Global Ecology* – This is the topmost level, and looks at how the sum of actions affects the planet as a whole. This could examine climate change, ozone levels in the atmosphere, warming of the oceans, etc.

2. *Ecosystem Ecology* – This level looks at large, similar regions. For example, much of northern Canada is tundra, a type of ecosystem. Ecosystem ecology would look at populations within the ecosystem and changes in available food or the food chain.

3. *Community Ecology* – This level of ecology looks at one particular area and the influence of different species in that area. For example, if a pack of wolves (a community) were introduced into a local forest, they would change the ecosystem.

4. *Population Ecology* – This is the lowest level of ecological study and concerns itself with the population of a single species within an environment.

Global Climate Change

One of the most important issues facing humanity today is our planet's changing climate. There is a broad scientific consensus that the earth is warming, and that human activity is the cause. The Earth's average temperature has increased by 0.8 °C since the year 1900, and is projected to warm up to 2-3 °C more by the year 2100. This is due to the production of anthropogenic greenhouse gases (anthropogenic = coming from people) - these include:

- *Carbon dioxide*: produced from burning of fossil fuels

- *Methane*: produced from livestock and the extraction of natural gas

- *NO_x compounds*: produced from industry and the burning of fossil fuels

These compounds, if present in the atmosphere, provide an insulating effect, as seen in the diagram below:

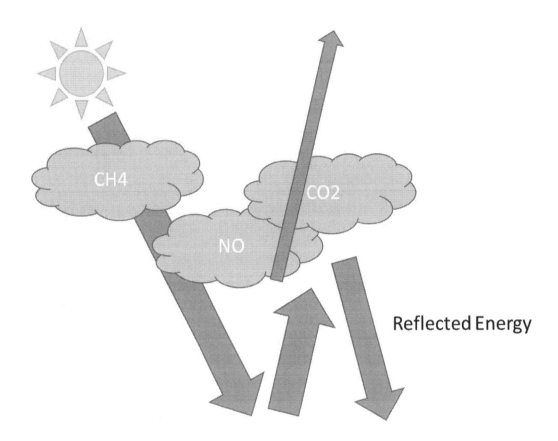

In the diagram above, sunlight enters the Earth's atmosphere, and a large portion of it is partially absorbed by biomass and other substances on the Earth's surface. However, due to the presence of greenhouse gas, a significant portion of the energy is again reflected back to the Earth, in an insulating process.

Note that without greenhouse gases, the Earth would not be able to retain much heat, and the temperature on the surface would drop significantly. Thus, greenhouse gases are required for comfortable conditions for life on Earth, but too much will result in droughts, vast crop shortages, widespread species extinction and other ecological catastrophes.

Types of Ecosystems

Ecosystems are typically defined by their climate, which is the average temperature and precipitation in the area. The pattern of temperature and precipitation also affects the definition of an ecosystem. There are eight major types, categorized in the table below.

Ecosystem	Characteristics
Tropical Forest	Typically moist and warm, with average temperatures year round of 25-29 C, and receiving 150-200 cm of precipitation every year. Tropical forests have a large number of species and are the most species-dense of all the ecosystems.
Desert	Deserts are the opposite of the rainforest, with temperatures varying widely between day and night. Daytime temperatures can exceed 45 C, and nighttime temperatures can fall below 30 C. Average precipitation is less than 30 cm every year. There is not much plant or animal life in the desert, but most plant life is either C4 or CAM-type plants.
Savanna	The savanna is best characterized as grassland, with rainfall between 30-50 cm every year and warm temperatures between 24-29 C. Savanna is the most typical ecosystem in Africa and some parts of northern China and southern Russia.
Chaparral	Chaparral is an ecosystem characterized by shrubs and low trees. A temperature ecosystem, it features rocky soil and low, rolling hills.

Temperate Grassland	This ecosystem typically receives 40-60 cm of seasonal precipitation every year. There are well-defined seasons, with temperatures in the summer rising above 30 C, and temperatures in the winter below 0. Temperate grassland is seen in the Midwest of the United States.
Coniferous Forest	Perhaps the most common type of forest, coniferous forest is seen in large parts of North America, Asia, and Europe. It is characterized by moderately cold temperatures, with an average year-round temperature around 15 C. It features plentiful coniferous trees, such as pine, hemlock, or spruce.
Broadleaf Forest	Broadleaf forests, containing many deciduous trees, are found in Europe and the eastern half of the United States. This ecosystem receives 70-150 cm of precipitation yearly.
Tundra	Tundra is one of the world's largest land area ecosystems, covering 20% of the world's existing land mass. It is quite cold, with temperatures usually no higher than 10 C, even in the summer. The tundra ecosystem is seen in northern Canada and northern Russia.

In addition to land ecosystems, there are also aquatic ecosystems. These include lakes, oceans, wetlands, streams, rivers, and estuaries.

Lakes	Lakes are small bodies of water completely enclosed by land. There is a varied level of salinity, but most lakes have a concentration of salt less than 0.5%. Lakes have a wide variety of life, and can support angiosperm plant life, which is rarely found in the ocean.

Wetlands	Wetlands, or swamps, are an area of land permeated with shallow water. In wetlands, there is a high concentration of microbes in the soil and water, resulting in low levels of dissolved oxygen in the water, and few fish species.
Streams & Rivers	Streams and rivers are interconnected aquatic habitats that lead to a lake or ocean. The water is high in oxygen and is usually free of salt. Many fish species live in streams and rivers, and are a good source of food for nearby predators.
Estuaries	Estuaries are regions that flow from the river into the sea. They are characterized by low beds of silt and sand. Many invertebrate crustaceans live in this zone.
Tidal Zones	A rocky or sandy area between the low and high ocean tide, home to many crustaceans.
Ocean Pelagic Zone	The ocean pelagic zone is found more than 500m off of the coastline, reaching depths of up to 10,000m. A wide variety of life exists in this zone.
Coral Reefs	Coral reefs are a unique biome created by corals, which form a calcium carbonate shell. Coral reefs are believed to have one of the highest species densities in the ocean. They can house many different types of fish, crustaceans, and single celled organisms.

Benthic zone	The benthic zone is the deep ocean, well below 10,000m. It receives no light, and lacks cyanobacteria and algae. However, there are extremophile species able to tolerate the high pressure and heat in areas near volcanic vents.

Population ecology examines a single group of individuals in a species. A population is defined as a group of organisms of the same species that lives in the same geographic area. For example, a population of lions might live in an area of savanna measuring roughly 30 square miles in Africa. The density of a population is the number of organisms found in an area, and the dispersion of a population is the pattern in which the organisms are spread.

Demographic Studies

Demographic studies are useful to understand a population's characteristics and the environmental factors that affect it. Life Tables are one measure of demographics that examines a population. In a life table, the population is examined at large, measuring the number that survives each year, passes away, or reproduces. This data can then be used to plot something called a survivorship curve, which shows the percentage of a certain population that survives over time.

Another important demographic for understanding a population is the reproduction rate. Researchers can measure the average number of offspring seen in a population to estimate the reproduction rate. Additionally, this rate can be affected by the number of females in the population. The rate of growth of a population can be used in the following equation:

$$P = A \times (1 + r)^n$$

In this equation, P is the present population, A is the starting population, r is the reproduction rate, and n is the number of years. This equation can be used to predict the number of individuals after a certain period.

Example:

If a population of squirrels reproduces at a rate of 4% per month, and the starting population is 50 squirrels, how many squirrels will there be after two years?

We fill in the equation to get:

$$P = 50 \times (1 + 0.04)^{24}$$

Note that *n* is 24 because we have 12 months in a year, and the period is two years. We find that after two years, we have 128 squirrels - the population has more than doubled.

Of course, populations do not usually expand exponentially. Death rates, diseases, predators, and other environmental factors will reduce the overall growth rate of a population. In fact, in many species, the population will usually only grow slightly or remain stable, due to the interaction of all the environmental variables.

One important environmental variable is called an "environment carrying capacity." This limits the maximum size of a population. For instance, a bacterial colony will enter a stationary phase and then a death phase after a certain number of bacteria have been produced. A similar thing will happen with animals, plants, fish, etc., as well. This is due to the limited number of resources present in an ecosystem. For example, if a sparrow eats 40 seeds per day, but the ecosystem nearby only produces 2000 seeds per day, then the maximum number of sparrows that can live in that ecosystem is 50. If the population grows beyond that amount, food stress will occur, eventually resulting in some sparrows dying.

Practice Examinations

Exam I

Multiple Choice

1. **Different organisms obtain their energy from different sources. For example, plants are autotrophs and create their own food, whereas most animals are heterotrophs, eating other organisms for energy. However, all of this energy is derived from:**

    A. Kinetic energy

    B. Light energy

    C. Adenosine tri-phosphate

    D. Bond energy

2. **In the diagram below, the cell could be best classified as a:**

    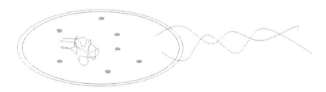

    A. Eukaryote

    B. Virus

    C. Blood cell

    D. Moneran

3. A scientist believes that algae are able to grow even when living deep underwater, but depending on the absorption of light by water and the presence of other algae, may grow more slowly than that found on the surface. Which of the following experimental findings would disprove the scientist's hypothesis?

    A. Algae and other protists are found to live more than 1000 meters under the surface of the water.

    B. Light is found to exponentially decrease in intensity underwater, such that there is no light existent beyond 50 meters underwater.

    C. Algae are found to grow in heavy mats on the ocean surface.

    D. Some species of algae are discovered that do not need much light to grow.

4. A farmer breeds tulips, and he wants to have one field grow only red tulips. Red tulips are a dominant allele (R), with the recessive allele (r) producing white tulips, and Rr producing red as well. Currently, 7/8 of his field is red, and $1/8^{th}$ is white. What can he do to produce only red tulips, and approximately how many generations must pass before more than 99% of his crop is red tulips?

    A. Remove all the white tulips, one generation.

    B. Remove all the white tulips and half of the red tulips, three generations.

    C. Remove all the white tulips, three generations.

    D. Remove all the white tulips and half of the red tulips, one generation.

5. **In the G protein-coupled receptor-signaling pathway, an external ligand binds to the exterior of the cell onto the receptor, as seen below. What happens next?**

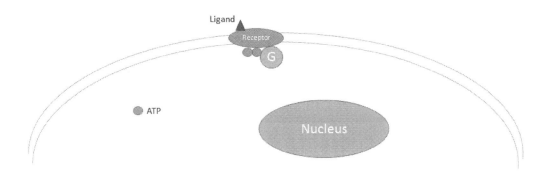

A. ATP is consumed to produce ADP, which acts as the signal to the nucleus.

B. A conformational change occurs that releases the G-protein, which acts as the intracellular signal.

C. The G-protein becomes active after hydrolyzing ATP, and attaches to the nucleus.

D. The receptor absorbs the ligand, which binds to the G-protein, activating it.

6. **Which of the following statements regarding life on earth is *not* true?**

A. The major elements in living organisms are carbon, oxygen, nitrogen, and silicon.

B. Many living creatures consume the remains of other organisms to acquire organic carbon.

C. Trace elements, such as iron, potassium, or sulfur, are required by a majority of living organisms.

D. Plants provide the major source of carbon for the kingdom Animalia.

7. Water is a unique molecule vital to life on earth. Which of the following properties is *not* a property of water that contributes to its usefulness?

    A. A high heat capacity

    B. A high surface tension

    C. Its liquid state across a wide variety of temperatures

    D. Its ability to degrade toxins

Questions 8 – 10 refer to the following information.

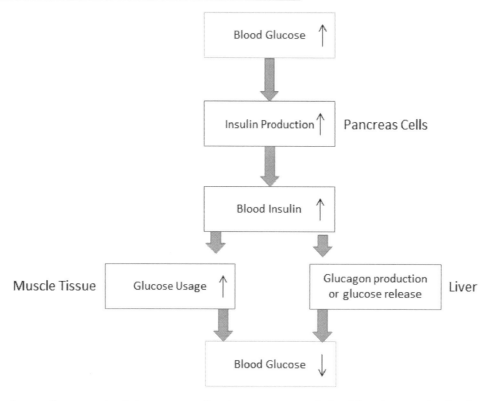

The above diagram depicts a generalized response path for blood sugar in the human body. The arrows represent increases.

8. **Which of the following statements is true, based on the diagram?**

    A. As blood insulin increases, blood sugar increases.

    B. In order for muscle tissue to use glucose, blood insulin must decrease.

    C. The liver can store glucose by hydrolyzing glucagon.

    D. If blood sugar increases, insulin production by pancreas cells leads eventually to blood sugar decreasing again.

9. **Diabetes Type I is a genetic disease in which the beta-islet cells in the pancreas are destroyed by an autoimmune response. For a person suffering from Type I diabetes who is not being treated, which of the following is correct?**

    A. Their blood sugar levels are usually very low

    B. Their blood sugar levels are usually very high

    C. Their muscle cells are incapable of using glucose

    D. Their liver is incapable of storing glucose as glucagon

10. **Alex is a diabetic, and takes insulin shots daily. One day, he accidentally took double his normal dose of insulin. This would cause his:**

    A. Muscles to overproduce energy

    B. Liver to fail

    C. Blood glucose to plummet

    D. Pancreas cells to produce more insulin

11. **Proteins have a tertiary structure that represents their three-dimensional structure. The tertiary structure is primarily held together by what kind of bond?**

    A. Di-sulfide bond

    B. Van der Waal's bond

    C. Ionic bond

    D. Polar bond

12. **Which of the following is an example of homoplasy?**

    A. The fact that salmon and tuna both have gills.

    B. The ability of multiple types of plants to grow in a rainforest.

    C. The ability of both birds and butterflies to fly.

    D. The many different species of elephants that exist.

13. A student is growing a sample of *Cryptococcus curvatus*, a yeast, in an incubator. He plotted a chart of the cell count over a period of days, and obtained the results seen below.

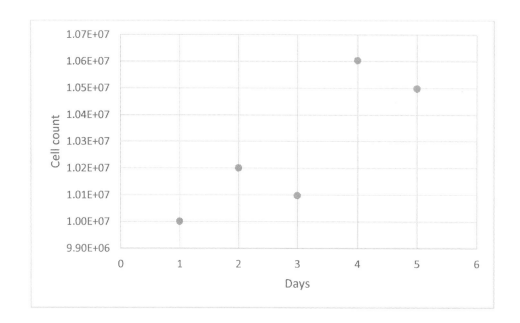

Which phase of growth are the yeast cells in?

    A. Exponential phase

    B. Growth phase

    C. Stationary phase

    D. Death phase

14. **Which of the following is *not* a cellular respiration pathway?**

    A. Glycolysis

    B. Citric acid cycle

    C. Entner-Doudoroff pathway

    D. Phosphoric shunt

15. **NADH and NAD+ are two molecules that are involved in the exchange of energy or electrons. When NAD+ becomes recycled into NADH, it is being:**

    A. Reduced

    B. Oxidized

    C. Hydrolyzed

    D. Galvanized

16. **Organisms obtain energy either autotrophically or heterotrophically. This energy is primarily used in:**

    A. Anabolic pathways

    B. Catabolic pathways

    C. Replicative pathways

    D. Polymeric pathways

17. **According to the following chart showing reducing potential, which of the following statements is true?**

$$ATP > NADH > FADH_2 > FADH+ > NAD+ > ADP$$

    A. FADH+ has a greater reduction potential than NADH

    B. FADH+, NAD+, and ADP are all electron donators

    C. ATP has the highest reducing potential and is thus the most likely to accept an electron.

    D. NADH and $FADH_2$ are less likely to donate electrons than ATP.

18. The thylakoid membrane structures, found only in organisms with chlorophyll, are the sites that:

    A. Produce ATP from sugar, much like mitochondria.

    B. Trap energy from the sun in the form of NADH and ATP.

    C. Provide an active site for the enzyme RuBisCo to fix carbon dioxide.

    D. Act as a structural platform from which the plant cell wall is generated.

19. There are many things wrong with the reaction below, describing the fixation of carbon dioxide. Which of the following is one of them?

$$6\ CO_2 + 6H_2O \xrightarrow{\text{RuBisCo, NADH}} C_6H_{12}O_6 + 6O_2$$

    A. RuBisCo requires an additional enzyme, anhydrase, in order to produce glucose.

    B. The formula for glucose should be $C_6H_{12}O_{12}$, and the energy source is ATP.

    C. RuBisCo produces 3-phosphoglycerate, not glucose, and does not use water.

    D. Oxygen is not a byproduct of carbon fixation. Instead, carbon monoxide (CO) is produced.

20. Which of the following is correct regarding the relationship between photosystem I and II?

A. Electrons are trapped by photosystem I, and proceed to photosystem II.

B. Photosystem I and II both trap electrons, but only photosystem II produces ATP.

C. Photosystem II traps energy from the sun to excite electrons, which are then provided to photosystem I.

D. Photosystem I is located in the cytosol, whereas photosystem II is located in the chloroplasts.

21. In the cross below, assuming perfect Mendelian inheritance, what percentage of the offspring will be tall and yellow?

Tall = T   TtGG   x   TTgg
Short = t

Green = G
Yellow = g

A. 0%

B. 12.5%

C. 25%

D. 50%

22. The Golgi body is one of the largest organelles found in the cell, and is responsible for:

A. Protein synthesis

B. Intracellular and extracellular transport

C. Replication of DNA

D. Formation of ribosomes

23. After a neuron cell accepts a signal, gated ion channels open in the cell, allowing an influx of sodium ions. This will cause which of the following to immediately occur?

    A. Cell potential to become more positive

    B. Cell potential to become more negative

    C. The neuron cell will start synthesizing transmitter proteins

    D. The neuron cell will pulse

24. Histone proteins can be found in which of these locations?

    A. Eukaryotic cell nucleus

    B. Prokaryotic cell nucleus

    C. Mitochondria

    D. All of the above

25. A scientist takes DNA samples from a cell culture at two different times, each sample having the same cell count. In the first sample, he finds that there is 6.5 pg of DNA, whereas in the second sample he finds that there is 13 pg of DNA. Which stage of the cell cycle is the second sample in?

    A. Interphase H

    B. Interphase S

    C. Prophase

    D. Interphase G2

26. If the gene AaBb is crossed by AAbb, how many different offspring genotypes are possible?

    A. 2

    B. 4

    C. 8

    D. 16

In a type of plant newly discovered in South America, the seed color is controlled by the gene R. In these plants, those having the dominant allele R have bright red seeds, and those that have the homozygous recessive allele pair *rr* have pale pink seeds. In the first generation, a scientist crosses a true-breeding RR plant with a recessive rr plant. The F1 plant is then crossed with itself, resulting in the F2 generation.

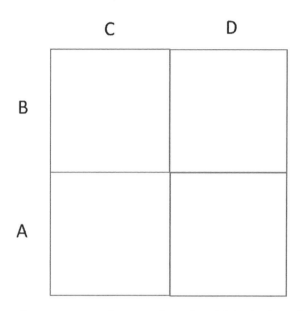

27. In the Punnett Square seen above, what should A, B, C, and D represent, respectively?

    A. R, r, R, r

    B. R, R, r, r

    C. r, r, R, r

    D. R, R, r, R

28. In the F2 generation, what percentage of the plants will have bright red seeds?

    A. 25%

    B. 50%

    C. 75%

    D. 100%

29. In the F1 generation, what percentage of the plants will be true breeding?

    A. 0%

    B. 25%

    C. 50%

    D. 75%

30. Which of the following processes will take place in both mitosis and meiosis?

    A. Separation of homologous chromatids

    B. Formation of new nuclei that each have half the number of chromosomes that exist in the parent nuclei.

    C. Production of chiasma during synapsis

    D. Separation of duplicated sister chromatids

31. During DNA replication, the 3' strand and the 5' strand are simultaneously replicated. Which enzyme is responsible for replicated the 3' strand?

    A. DNA polymerase III

    B. DNA ligase

    C. DNA polymerase I

    D. DNA helicase

32. A scientist is trying to clone a gene for insertion into *E. coli*. However, she is finding that when she uses a polymerase chain reaction to duplicate the gene, she is not making any new DNA at all! Which of the following could be the problem?

    A. She has forgotten to add DNA nucleotides to her mixture.

    B. She has forgotten to add intron primer to her mixture.

    C. Her temperature of annealing of 55 °C is too low.

    D. Her temperature of denaturation of 95 °C is too high.

33. Which of the following statements is *not true* regarding the structure of DNA?

    A. DNA is held together primarily by covalent bonds.

    B. The DNA structure is helical.

    C. DNA is comprised of four subunits: adenine, uracil, guanine, and cytosine.

    D. The DNA backbone is comprised party of sugar.

34. In the diagram shown below, which block of DNA is most likely to be a promoter sequence for the transcribed area (shown in red)?

    A. A

    B. B

    C. C

    D. D

35. Turtles and fish both eat insects and small fish in streams or lakes. Because of this, they could be described as:

    A. Symbiotic

    B. Occupying the same niche

    C. In the same family

    D. Biological producers

36. A plant that exhibits a trait called phototropism will be:

    A. Turned to face the sun.

    B. Able to grow upside down.

    C. Able to produce its own food.

    D. Turned to face a source of heat.

37. The following figure is indicative of which type of population distribution?

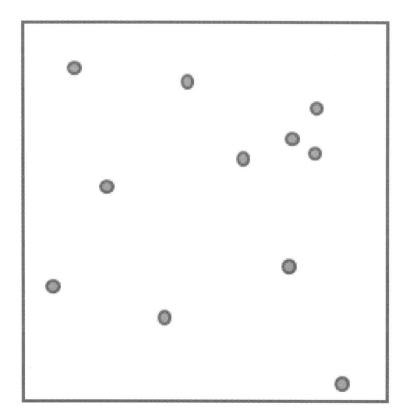

    A. Clumped

    B. Random

    C. Disperse

    D. Ring

38. A nucleosome is a structure of tightly packed DNA, allowing for eventual formation into chromatids. What are nucleosomes wrapped around?

    A. Ribosomes

    B. DNA polymerase

    C. Histones

    D. Telomeres

39. The chart below shows the population demographics of Littletown, USA. Which of the following is true about the population in this town?

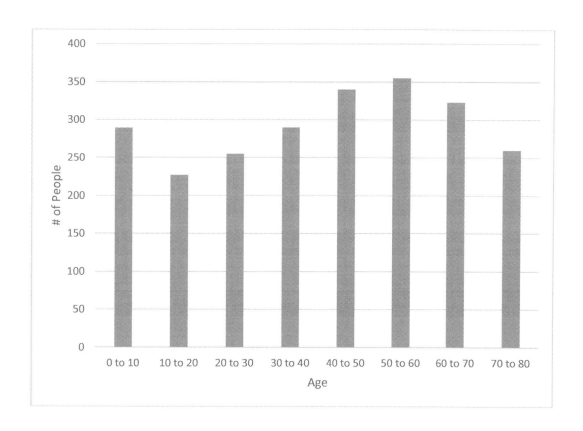

A. It has a growing population

B. It has little to no population growth

C. It has a decreasing population

D. It has an exponentially expanding population

40. Which of the following is an example of a primary consumer in the food chain?

A. Ant

B. Fish

C. Hawk

D. Tree

41. A student is taking a field trip to explore a new biome. The area that he is visiting has sparse trees, many grasses, and a moderate temperature year-round. Which of these biomes could he be visiting?

    A. Rainforest

    B. Desert

    C. Temperate Deciduous Forest

    D. Savanna

42. The translation process, in which DNA is read and translated into mRNA and then into an amino acid sequence, requires all of the following except:

    A. tRNA

    B. snRNP's

    C. Amino acids

    D. RNA polymerase

43. In the figure below, a DNA strand and its complementary strand is shown:

    DNA template strand   5' _____ 3'

    DNA complementary strand   3' _____ 5'

    Assuming the DNA strand is unwound and prepared for transcription to mRNA, which strand does the RNA polymerase attach to, and in which direction does it transcribe the DNA?

    A. Template strand, 5' to 3'

    B. Template strand, 3' to 5'

    C. Complementary strand, 5' to 3'

    D. Complementary strand, 3' to 5'

Questions 44 to 45 refer to the codon table below:

Standard genetic code

1st base	2nd base								3rd base
	T		C		A		G		
T	TTT	(Phe/F) Phenylalanine	TCT	(Ser/S) Serine	TAT	(Tyr/Y) Tyrosine	TGT	(Cys/C) Cysteine	T
	TTC		TCC		TAC		TGC		C
	TTA	(Leu/L) Leucine	TCA		TAA	Stop (Ochre)	TGA	Stop (Opal)	A
	TTG		TCG		TAG	Stop (Amber)	TGG	(Trp/W) Tryptophan	G
C	CTT	(Leu/L) Leucine	CCT	(Pro/P) Proline	CAT	(His/H) Histidine	CGT	(Arg/R) Arginine	T
	CTC		CCC		CAC		CGC		C
	CTA		CCA		CAA	(Gln/Q) Glutamine	CGA		A
	CTG		CCG		CAG		CGG		G
A	ATT	(Ile/I) Isoleucine	ACT	(Thr/T) Threonine	AAT	(Asn/N) Asparagine	AGT	(Ser/S) Serine	T
	ATC		ACC		AAC		AGC		C
	ATA		ACA		AAA	(Lys/K) Lysine	AGA	(Arg/R) Arginine	A
	ATG[A]	(Met/M) Methionine	ACG		AAG		AGG		G
G	GTT	(Val/V) Valine	GCT	(Ala/A) Alanine	GAT	(Asp/D) Aspartic acid	GGT	(Gly/G) Glycine	T
	GTC		GCC		GAC		GGC		C
	GTA		GCA		GAA	(Glu/E) Glutamic acid	GGA		A
	GTG		GCG		GAG		GGG		G

44. Which of the following DNA sequences coding for an amino acid sequence does *not* include a stop codon?

    A. TTG-GTC-TAA-AAT

    B. TTT-GGC-AGA-CTC

    C. GTA-AUG-TAG-AGC

    D. TTC-CAT-CAC-TGC

45. A researcher has discovered a mutation in a sequence of DNA, which changes a codon from AGG to ATG. What effect will this have on the sequence?

    A. There will be no effect.

    B. The codon sequence will start being translated at a different location than before.

    C. The codon sequence will stop being translated at a different location than before.

    D. The protein will no longer fold at all due to the mismatched codon.

46. In order for genetic drift to occur, in which a gene allele drops out of the population, which of the following must be true of the population?

 A. The population is large

 B. The population is small

 C. The population has many food sources

 D. The population is able to survive in many niches

The following information is required to answer questions 47 – 48.

Sickle cell anemia is a recessive trait that causes red blood cells to be curved, or sickle shaped. As a result, these blood cells are unable to carry as much oxygen as normal red blood cells. In the global population, the sickle cell anemia trait is present in only 0.2% of humans. However, in Sub-Saharan Africa, where malaria is common, up to 4% of the population possesses sickle-cell anemia.

47. Which of the following is a hypothesis that connects the sickle-cell anemia trait to malaria?

 A. Based on the increased incidence of sickle cell anemia in areas where malaria is prevalent, malaria increases the percentage of the population that has sickle cell anemia.

 B. Based on the increased incidence of malaria in areas where sickle cell anemia is present, malaria is more apt to infect those who have the dominant allele for sickle-cell anemia.

 C. Based on the increased incidence of malaria in Sub-Saharan Africa, sickle-cell anemia evolved to combat malaria.

 D. None of the above hypotheses are correct.

48. If 4% of the population possesses sickle-cell anemia, what percentage of alleles in the gene pool are the sickle-cell alleles?

 A. 4%

 B. 12%

 C. 20%

 D. 24%

49. The chart below shows a graph of the number of people at each height in a given population. Which of the following is true about this population based on this graph?

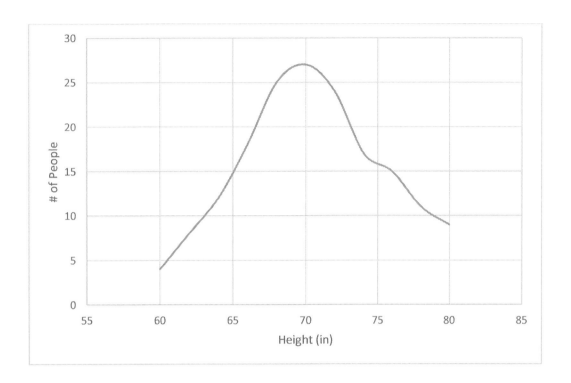

A. The population has undergone mutation

B. The population has undergone stabilizing selection

C. The population has undergone positive selection

D. The population has undergone recessive selection

50. Salivary amylase is secreted by the saliva glands in your mouth, especially when you eat what kind of food?

A. Foods high in protein

B. Foods high in starch

C. Foods high in fat

D. Foods high in fiber

51. In humans, which organ is not part of the endocrine system?

    A. The stomach

    B. The pancreas

    C. The hypothalamus

    D. The pineal gland

52. A Barr body is an unusual formation of a high-density clump of inactivated DNA. Where might you find a Barr body?

    A. Any gamete cell

    B. A male sex cell

    C. A female sex cell

    D. A female somatic cell

53. Which of the following is not a greenhouse gas?

    A. Carbon dioxide

    B. Nitrous oxide

    C. Methane

    D. Helium

54. If a trait is recessively linked to the X-chromosome, then it will most likely be seen in:

    A. Males

    B. Females

    C. Both genders

    D. Neither gender

55. A scientist is examining the crossover rate of a series of genes on the same chromosome. He finds that their crossover rates are as below in the table:

A - D	55%
B - C	15%
C - A	30%
A - B	10%

What is the correct order of genes on the chromosome?

    A. A B C D

    B. A C D B

    C. B D C A

    D. C A B D

56. Which of the following is not an element commonly found in living organisms?

    A. Carbon

    B. Phosphorus

    C. Potassium

    D. Titanium

57. Which of the following statements regarding the human chromosomes is *not* true?

    A. Humans have 23 pairs of chromosomes

    B. Humans have the most chromosomes out of any species

    C. Chromosomal genes can cross-over with each other

    D. Only one set of chromosomes is present in each gamete cell

58. In animal cell structure, the cell membrane is composed of a phospholipid bilayer that separates the cell from its surroundings. Which of the following is also present in the cell membrane?

   A. Proteins

   B. ATP

   C. Mitochondria

   D. Vacuoles

59. A student places a cell with a 50 mM intracellular ion content into a solution containing 20 mM ion content. What will happen to the cell?

   A. The cell will shrink

   B. The cell membrane will become porous

   C. The cell will expand

   D. The cell is isotonic, and nothing will occur

60. Transportation of molecules into the cell is governed by all of the following except:

   A. Cell surface area

   B. Transport proteins in the membrane

   C. Receptor-mediated transport channels

   D. Fatty-acid chain import

Grid-In Questions

(6 Questions)

1. **After fertilization of an egg, cell division begins. After six divisions, how many cells exist in the embryo?**

   Answer ____________

2. **In a given population following the Hardy-Weinberg equilibrium, it was discovered that 2,350 people were heterozygous for the red hair trait, with the gene alleles Rr. Roughly how many people have the double recessive gene alleles rr?**

   Answer____________

3. **A population of crabs is discovered to have a growth rate of 9.5% every year during years in which they are fished, and a growth rate of 25.8% every year that they are not. If their starting population is 5,000, and they are fished the first year, what is their population after five years?**

   Answer____________

4. **In a certain ecosystem, about 2000 kg of plant biomass is produced monthly. If all 2000 kg of this mass is consumed by primary consumers, approximately what is the mass of primary consumers produced monthly?**

   Answer____________

5. **A man and a woman have had four girls in a row. What is the probability that their fifth child will also be a girl?**

   Answer____________

6. In the cross AaBb x AAbb, what percentage of offspring will have the double recessive allele bb?

Answer_____

Free Response

Problems 1-2 are long answer. Problems 3-8 are short answer, and should be answered in no more than two short paragraphs.

1. **A student conducts an experiment on the oleaginous yeast *Cryptococcus curvatus*. During the course of the experiment, the student grows the species on two sugar substrates: glucose and xylose (a 5-carbon sugar), over a range of temperatures from 10°C to 75 °C, and measures the production of lipid. He obtains the results seen below:**

Glucose Substrate	Temp	10	20	30	40	50	60	75
	Lipid Content (mg)	7	8	17	21	16	5	1.5

Xylose Substrate	Temp	10	20	30	40	50	60	75
	Lipid Content (mg)	2	2.8	3.1	1.3	0.7	0	0

   a. Draw a chart with the data from both tables plotted onto it.

   b. Based on the data shown, what is a conclusion for the effect of temperature on lipid production?

   c. Propose a theory for the difference between the growth rates seen in the glucose and the xylose substrates.

2. **Transportation of substances across a cell membrane is vital to the life of a cell, and there are many methods of transferring molecules across the membrane.**

   a. Describe two types of cellular transport processes in detail, including energy required, cellular structures involved, and types of molecules transferred.

3. Enzymes are important structures that control many reactions in the human body, and are composed of different amino acid sequences.

   a. How is the structure of an enzyme related to DNA?

   b. A scientist has a hypothesis that temperatures greater than the temperatures in the human body (37 °C), will cause proteins and enzymes to denature. Design an experiment that could prove or disprove this hypothesis.

4. In aerobic respiration, sugar is broken down to create ATP, NADH, and other byproducts. As a result, CO_2 and water are produced. In aerobic respiration, oxygen is the terminal electron acceptor. Describe the process of electron transport through aerobic respiration, and postulate how a different element, such as sulfate, could be used as a terminal electron acceptor as a replacement for oxygen.

5. **In the diagram below, the X-axis represents the number of hours for an algal growth culture, and the Y-axis represents the cell count.**

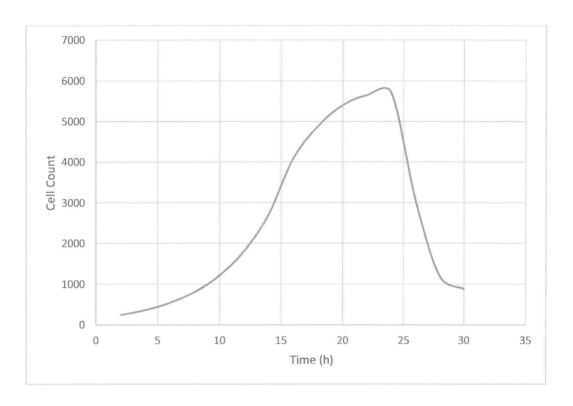

    a. Describe what is happening between hour 10 and hour 24.

    b. Propose an explanation for the sharp cell count drop after the 24th hour of growth.

6. **Explain the Hardy-Weinberg equilibrium theory and why it is or is not applicable to real-world situations.**

7. **Genetic variation is one of the driving factors of evolution and natural selection. Name and describe two factors that can cause genetic variation.**

8. **Ferns are unique plants that do not reproduce using flowers or seeds. Draw a diagram outlining the reproductive cycle of a fern, and in a short paragraph, explain the main distinctions between ferns and traditional plants that reproduce using seeds.**

Answer Key

Multiple Choice

1. B	20. C	40. A
2. D	21. A	41. D
3. B	22. B	42. B
4. C	23. A	43. B
5. B	24. A	44. C
6. A	25. D	45. B
7. D	26. B	46. B
8. D	27. A	47. A
9. B	28. C	48. C
10. C	29. A	49. B
11. A	30. D	50. B
12. C	31. C	51. A
13. C	32. A	52. D
14. D	33. C	53. D
15. A	34. C	54. A
16. A	35. B	55. A
17. D	36. A	56. D
18. B	37. B	57. B
19. C	38. C	58. A
	39. B	59. C
		60. D

Grid-In

1. Sixty-four cells will exist after six divisions. The calculation performed is 2^6. Each division doubles the number of cells.

2. 1175 people will have the double recessive trait. In the Hardy-Weinberg equilibrium, gene counts remain stable. Generally, when given the number of heterozygous allele pairs in a population, it is known that the number of double recessive allele pairs is half that amount.

3. The starting population is 5,000. The first year, they are fished, and have a growth rate of 9.5%. This then alternates every other year for four more years.

$$5,000*(1.095)^3*(1.258)^2 = 10389 \text{ crabs}$$

4. From each tier of the food chain, about 10% of consumed mass is turned into actual mass. Thus, if 2000 kg of producer mass is consumed, this will equate to about 200 kg of primary consumer mass.

5. 50%. Regardless of previous events, the probability for an independent event is the same. Thus, the chance to have a girl is 50%.

6. In this question, we can ignore the "A" alleles. Looking at the B alleles, a Bb x bb will have 50% Bb and 50% bb.

Free Response

1. The graph should look as seen below:

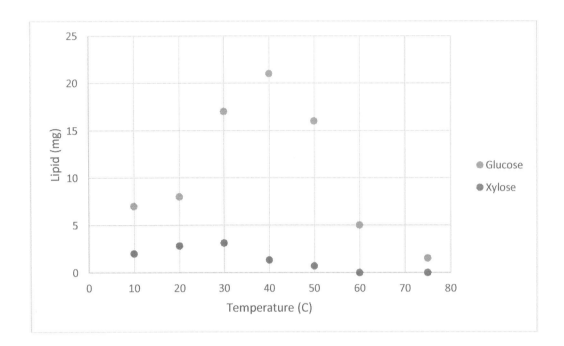

Main points that need to be addressed in the remaining parts:

a. The student should determine that the optimum growth rate is between 35 to 40 degrees C. They should also mention that warmer or colder temperatures might have an effect on the rate of respiration, due to the activity of enzymes at different temperatures.

b. The student should talk about the use of glucose by yeast and examine the possible different pathways between a C6 sugar (glucose) and a C5 sugar (xylose). They should talk about the usual pathway for breakdown of a C6 sugar in yeast and propose some reasons why it does not work well for a C5 sugar. This should then be linked to decreased lipid production rate seen in the xylose-fed yeast.

2. The student has three primary options to choose from: passive transport (diffusion or osmosis), active transport (protein or gate mediated transport), and endo- or exocytosis (vacuole transport).

   a. Passive transport main points

      i. Requires no energy

      ii. Requires a concentration gradient

      iii. Can only transport small molecules, and not proteins

      iv. Diffusion refers to the transport of molecules, osmosis refers to the transport of water

   b. Active transport main points

      i. Requires energy, either ATP or NADH

      ii. Requires a signal of some sort, either extracellular signal binding or intracellular signal

      iii. Transport occurs through a gated channel in the membrane or is mediated by a cell membrane protein

      iv. Can transport larger molecules

   c. Endo/exocytosis main points

      i. Used to excrete waste from the cell

      ii. Occurs through the merging of a vacuole into the cell membrane

3. The student should focus on:

    a. The relationship between DNA and an enzyme. A description needs to be provided of the translation process from DNA to RNA, RNA to amino acid chain, then the folding of the AA chain into an enzyme.

    b. An experimental design needs to consist of:

        i. Replicated samples

        ii. Control samples

        iii. A tested (varied) factor, in this case temperature.

    For example, the scientist could set up an experiment in which there is a control sample not exposed to temperature, and then three replicated test samples: one at 45 C, one at 55 C, and one at 65 C. If the enzyme is denatured at the higher temperature and the control sample is not, then the hypothesis is proven true.

4. The main points the student needs to focus on:

    a. The pathway of electrons in the respiration pathway, i.e. a description of electrons as they pass from glucose to pyruvate to ATP and NADH, and then how ATP is used, etc.

    b. The fact that the terminal electron acceptor can be many different elements, but the ability of a material to act as a terminal electron acceptor depends on its reduction potential (oxygen has a very high reduction potential and is very suitable).

5. The main points that need to be mentioned:

    a. The growth cycle of microorganisms, going through a lag phase (until about six hours in this chart), the exponential phase (six to twenty hours), and the stationary phase.

    b. The student needs to mention that it is unusual for cells to experience such a rapid decline in number after 24 hours. Something must have happened to the solution, such as the addition of a chemical or toxin. Normally, after cells reach stationary phase, they will only slowly decline in number for a long while.

6. The main points that need to be mentioned:

   a. The Hardy-Weinberg equilibrium theory states that the allele count of a particular gene will remain stable throughout time. For example, if the frequency of one allele is 10%, it will stay at 10%.

   b. The student should state that HW equilibrium is NOT realistic. There are many assumptions that are required for HW to work. This includes non-random mating, no mutation, no environmental selection, no genetic drift or gene flow. The student should mention at least 2-3 of these assumptions.

7. The main points that need to be mentioned:

   a. Genetic variation primarily arises through sexual reproduction and mutation.

   b. Other sources include crossing over and random fertilization in a population.

8. The diagram should resemble and include the majority of the elements listed below:

   a. Spore -> young gametophyte -> antheridium -> zygote -> sporophyte -> fern -> sporangium formation -> spore

   b. Differences that should be noted

      i.   Ferns reproduce asexually compared to the majority of plants

      ii. Ferns alternate generations of haploid and diploid gametes

      iii. Ferns have no flowers and produce no seeds

Multiple Choice

1. **In the human testes, cells undergo meiosis to produce sperm. After the process of meiosis, how many chromosomes exist in the sperm cell?**

    A. 13

    B. 23

    C. 46

    D. 52

2. **In the theory of evolution, natural selection is partially driven by environmental factors. Which of the following factors might affect the selection of a gray field mouse?**

    A. The available food in the area increases due to recent rainfall.

    B. An invasive species introduced to the area that preys on the field mouse.

    C. A recent flood causes the environment to have more silt.

    D. None of the above will affect the field mouse's selection.

<u>Questions 3-5 refer to the following diagram of a plant leaf.</u>

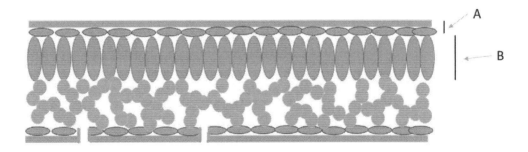

3. In the figure, what area of the plant leaf does 'B' refer to?

    A. Upper Epidermis

    B. Cell wall

    C. Palisade mesophyll

    D. Parenchyma

4. In the spongy mesophyll, seen as the lighter green cells in the diagram, there are many open spaces. These spaces are required for:

    A. Improve leaf structural stability

    B. Access to carbon dioxide for carbon fixing reactions

    C. Cooling of the plant

    D. Access for symbiotic insects

5. The stoma or stomata, seen as small gap cells in the cuticle of the cell wall, are usually located on the underside of the leaf. Which of the following is the correct reason for their location?

    A. To prevent excess loss of moisture

    B. To prevent insect attacks

    C. To prevent water from entering the leaf

    D. To allow greater flow of oxygen into the plant leaf

6. In the human circulatory system, where does blood progress after exiting the left ventricle?

    A. The right ventricle

    B. The aorta

    C. The pulmonary artery

    D. The left atrium

7. **Introns are non-coding regions of DNA that separate the codon regions, called exons. How are introns removed when a RNA transcript is made?**

   A. Through a promoter

   B. Function of the Poly-adenine tail on the intron region

   C. Use of GTP

   D. With a spliceosome

8. **Which of the following is *not* a chemical involved in the human immune response?**

   A. Prostaglandins

   B. Chemokines

   C. Erythrocytes

   D. Histamines

9. **A student is performing an experiment in which he adds a chemical that prevents hydrogen bond formation in a cell. As a result, the cell's proteins will have their:**

   A. Primary structure affected

   B. Secondary structure affected

   C. Excretion affected

   D. The cell's proteins will not be affected at all

10. In an experiment, a scientist grows a fungal culture in a media that contains ^{35}S, a slightly radioactive form of sulfur. He notices that at maturity, the fungal cells show a significant concentration of ^{35}S in the cell wall, as well as in the intracellular cytosol. Which of the following conclusions can be drawn from this finding?

    A. The fungus excretes enzymes or protein extra-cellularly.

    B. The fungus incorporates a significant amount of sulfur into its phospholipid bilayer.

    C. The fungus cell wall has many protein inclusions.

    D. The fungus uses sulfur as its terminal electron acceptor.

11. Cholesterol molecules are present in the cell membrane. What is their physiological function?

    A. Signal transduction from attached neurotransmitters

    B. Provides membrane fluidity.

    C. Allows the cell membrane to absorb more moisture.

    D. Enables the cell membrane to become more porous and allow diffusion.

12. The diagram below shows a tube separated at the bottom by a semi-permeable membrane. The concentrations of solutes on either side of the membrane are shown in the diagram. At equilibrium, what will be the concentration of Sodium on side B?

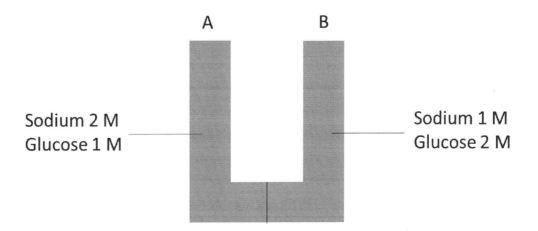

Sodium 2 M
Glucose 1 M

Sodium 1 M
Glucose 2 M

    A. 1 M

    B. 1.5 M

    C. 2 M

    D. 0 M

13. In a voltage-gated ion channel for sodium, a nerve impulse will cause the channel to open, allowing an influx of sodium that increases the cell's potential. What ion is then responsible for the restoration of the resting potential?

    A. Potassium

    B. Sodium

    C. Calcium

    D. Magnesium

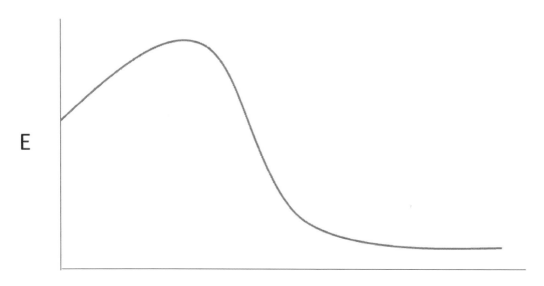

E

Reaction Progress

14. **What is represented by the first part of the curve that leads up to the peak?**

    A. The kinetic barrier

    B. The activation energy

    C. The heat energy

    D. The potential barrier

15. **Many reactions in the human body follow this type of energy curve, which would establish the reaction as being:**

    A. Endothermic

    B. 2nd order

    C. Exothermic

    D. In the aqueous phase

16. A scientist provides a growing sunflower plant with CO_2 that has been made with heavy oxygen, an isotope of normal oxygen that has a weight of 18 AMUs, rather than 16. After the carbon dioxide has been metabolized, where will the heavy oxygen show up?

    A. In water secreted by the plant.

    B. In glucose created by the plant.

    C. In pyruvate created by the plant.

    D. In oxygen produced by the plant.

17. In C4 plants, compared to C3, photorespiration does not appear to occur due to the action of which enzyme responsible for fixing CO_2?

    A. RuBisCO

    B. Glucose transferase

    C. Pyruvate dehydrogenase

    D. PEP carboxylase

18. Chlorophyll A absorbs light at a frequency of 460 nm to produce higher energy electrons. This light is:

    A. Green

    B. Blue

    C. Red

    D. White

Questions 19-20 are based on the following table, which represents the number of minutes spent in each stage of the cell cycle by three different types of eukaryotic cells.

Cell Type	G1 Phase	S Phase	G2 Phase	M Phase
Alpha	16	25	11	18
Beta	50	0	0	0
Zeta	16	51	15	19

19. Which of the following is true concerning the difference between Beta and Zeta cells in the S phase?

    A. The beta cells have more DNA than the zeta cells.

    B. The zeta cells have 51 times the amount of DNA than the beta cells.

    C. Neither of these cells reproduces sexually.

    D. The zeta cells have more DNA than the beta cells.

20. What is the best explanation for the fact that the Beta cells have no time spent in the S, G2, and M phases?

    A. They were in the G0 growth phase the entire time.

    B. These cells contain no DNA, and thus do not progress through the growth phases.

    C. These cells are in lag phase due to lack of nutrients.

    D. These cells have mismatched chromosomes and thus were unable to replicate at all.

21. **Nitrogen utilized by plants is fixed by microbes using enzymes and atmospheric nitrogen. What compound is produced?**

    A. $NO_3{}^{2-}$

    B. NH_2

    C. $NH_4{}^{+}$

    D. NKP

22. **Which of the following cellular processes does not use ATP?**

    A. Facilitated diffusion

    B. DNA replication

    C. Active transport through the cell membrane

    D. Movement of the *mot* complex in a flagellum

23. **In plants, the formation of a seed includes the creation of an endosperm. Which of the following is not true about the endosperm?**

    A. It can have a triploid (3n) chromosome number.

    B. The endosperm in many plants contains fats and nutrients for the growing embryo.

    C. The endosperm is created solely from maternal tissue.

    D. The endosperm begins formation after a pollen grain contacts the maternal cell.

24. **Viruses and prokaryotes both differ from eukaryotes in that they do not have a nuclear membrane. What is one manner in which viruses are distinguished from prokaryotes?**

    A. Viruses contain RNA, and prokaryotes do not.

    B. Prokaryotes have ribosomes, whereas viruses do not.

    C. Prokaryotes can form a protein shell, whereas viruses cannot.

    D. Viruses are harmful to humans, whereas prokaryotes are not.

25. Hemophilia is a sex-linked recessive trait predominantly seen in males. If a male inherits this disease, from whom does he get the recessive alleles?

   A. His mother only

   B. His father only

   C. Either the father or the mother

   D. The inheritance of this allele cannot be determined

26. Trees must move water from the roots all the way up to the top of the tree. Which of the following phenomena provides the most driving force for the movement of water up a tree?

   A. The surface tension of water

   B. Osmotic force

   C. Capillary action

   D. Transpiration/evaporation

27. A student goes on a wilderness exploration, and discovers what she thinks is a new plant. The plant has branched veins on the leaves, contains some small fruit, and possesses vascular bundles in its stem. This plant is similar to, and could be classified as a:

   A. Maize plant

   B. Fern

   C. Pine tree

   D. Pea plant

28. Which cell stage comes immediately after the morula stage of cell development?

   A. Blastula

   B. Blastocyst

   C. Eight-cell complex

   D. Embryo

29. The phenomenon of imprinting is typically found in:

    A. Lizard species

    B. Bird species

    C. Mammalian species

    D. Fish species

30. The phytochrome complex in plants is best known for its relationship in regulation of which of the following functions?

    A. Glycogen production

    B. Photoperiodism

    C. Phototropism

    D. Anther pollen production

31. The pink salmon typically spawn in the late summer, between July and September, whereas the sockeye salmon typically spawn between June and July. These two species do not usually reproduce with each other because of:

    A. Temporal isolation

    B. Habitat isolation

    C. Geographic isolation

    D. Physical isolation

32. A student is attempting to replicate the Miller-Urey experiment. Which of the following reagents does he *not* need?

    A. Ammonia

    B. Carbon dioxide

    C. Oxygen

    D. Water vapor

33. Temperature regulation is an important aspect of homeostasis in warm-blooded animals. In mammals, which of the following is *not* functional for temperature regulation?

    A. Sweating

    B. Large surface area ears

    C. Reduced blood flow to peripheral body parts

    D. Panting

Questions 34 to 35 refer to the following information:

Over a period of several hundred years, a glacier melts and is transformed into a lake. Later, the lake slowly dries up and becomes a valley, where grasses and shrubs predominantly grow. During the course of this time, different ecological communities come and go.

34. This passage describes which of the following ecological processes?

    A. Convergence

    B. Succession

    C. Niche creation

    D. Transformation

35. The number of species inhabiting this ecology since the beginning has likely:

    A. Increased

    B. Decreased

    C. Stayed the same

    D. Decreased first, and then increased

36. Which of the following is *not* true about the molecule seen below?

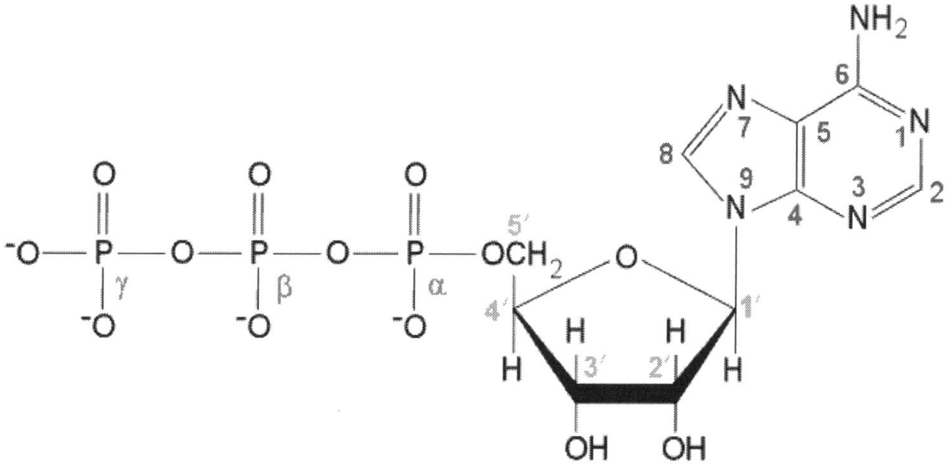

A. The molecule is called adenosine triphosphate

B. The molecule releases energy if one of the phosphate molecules is released

C. A polymerized form of this molecule is used for long term energy storage

D. The sugar unit in this molecule is the same as that found in RNA

37. Which of the following is not a compound created from sugar?

A. Glycogen

B. Starch

C. Cellulose

D. Guanine

38. If a gene allele is neither dominant nor recessive, it could be referred to as:

A. Pleotropic

B. Incompletely dominant

C. Crossed over

D. Homologous

39. In the domain Archaea, there are many species of unicellular organisms. Which of the following is a key difference between organisms in Archaea and Bacteria?

    A. Archaea cells do not contain peptidoglycan in their cell wall

    B. Archaea cells do not contain phospholipids in their cell membrane

    C. Archaea cells do not use RNA

    D. Archaea cells do not use ribosomes to produce amino acid chains

Questions 40 to 42 refer to the following passage and graph.

The chart depicts a graph of a patients antibody count during the course of an infection. The X-axis is the number of days, and the Y-axis is the antibody count in millimolars.

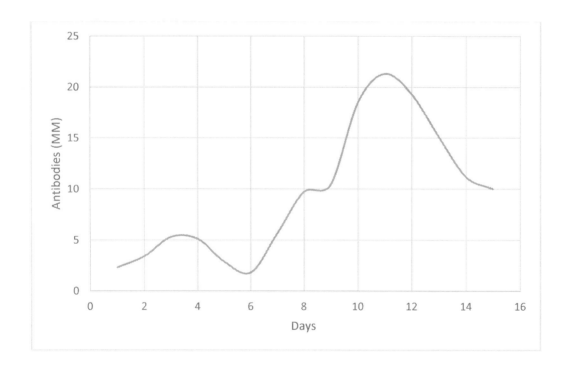

40. What is the likely cause of the initial increase of antibody count around day 5?

      A. The start of an antibiotic regimen

      B. Introduction of an MHC I or II compound

      C. Initial contact with an antigen

      D. A cut or scrape

41. The major immune response seen around day twelve, which produced a significant number of antibodies, is a result of the action of what type of white blood cell?

      A. B Cells

      B. T Cells

      C. Endocytic macrophages

      D. Erythrocytes

42. Which of the following is not usually found in lymph?

      A. T cells

      B. B cells

      C. Erythrocytes

      D. Plasma

43. A student recently planted an experimental garden, and used a lamp that emits 380 nm wavelength light at high intensity to promote growth. She watered the garden daily, but it did not grow well, and all the plants were sickly and weak. Which of the following could explain this?

      A. Plants use light around 450 nm, and not 380 nm.

      B. Plants cannot grow if exposed to constant light. They need some dark time.

      C. She likely watered the plants too much.

      D. The plants require light at 280 nm, not 380 nm.

44. In an biology lab, the students tested out different methods of sterilization. Based on the data seen in the table below, which of the following conclusions can be drawn?

METHOD	CELLS REMAINING
ULTRAVIOLET LIGHT	2.5×10^4
BOILING	1.9×10^5
BLEACH STERILIZATION	0.5×10^2
AUTOCLAVE	0.1×10

A. Boiling is the most effective method of sterilization.

B. Ultraviolet light is only slightly more effective than boiling.

C. Autoclaving is more than 200 times as effective compared to bleach sterilization.

D. All tested methods of sterilization were effective at removing a high percentage of cells.

45. The key function of topoisomerase in the DNA replication is to:

A. Unwind the DNA

B. Align the base pairs

C. Form the bond between annealing base pairs

D. Remove single nucleotide mutations

46. Which of the following must happen for allopatric speciation to occur?

A. A geographic separation

B. A change in available food

C. A bottleneck event

D. A temporal separation

47. Which box in the following Punnett Square is incorrectly filled out?

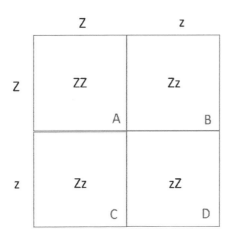

    A. A

    B. B

    C. C

    D. D

48. All of the following are signaling molecules of some sort, but which of these is used to relay a signal between neurons?

    A. GABA

    B. ATP

    C. Ca^{2+}

    D. Cl^-

49. Which part of a tree contains the most living material, and subsequently is used to transport water?

    A. Xylem

    B. Phloem

    C. Pith

    D. Heartwood

50. Which of the following species is classified into the producer trophic level?

    A. *Pinus radiata* (Monterey Pine)

    B. *Mus musculus* (House Mouse)

    C. *Sympetrum flaveolum* (Yellow Darter Dragonfly)

    D. *Cyptotrama chrysopeplum* (Yellow Cap Mushroom)

51. A detective arrives at a new crime scene, and proceeds to gather evidence. He needs to get a DNA sample. Which of the following samples would contain the least DNA?

    A. Saliva

    B. Red blood cells

    C. Hair

    D. Semen

52. A scientist discovers a new island, and finds what he believes to be a new species of cockroach. Upon gathering a respectable sample size of these cockroaches and testing their DNA, he finds that they have very little allele variation and almost the exact same phenotype. How is this possible?

    A. A population bottleneck event

    B. A speciation event

    C. A reverse founder effect

    D. This is not possible. An error must have occurred in sampling.

Questions 53 to 54 refer to the following passage and chart.

A scientist discovers a new species of snail that lives in the ocean. He tests the ability of this species to handle heat, and produces the data seen below. In the experiment, he tested the growth rate of the species as he increased the temperature of the water in which it lived. He also tested two different concentrations of salt, in accordance with the species' ability to live in the ocean.

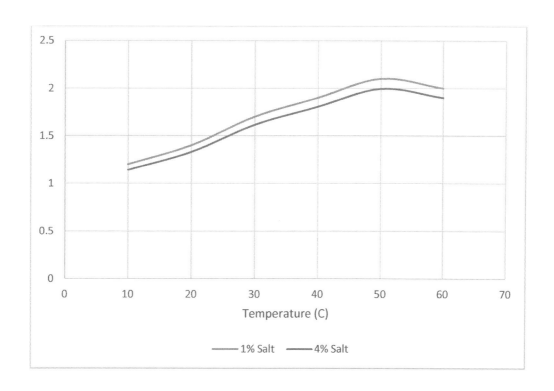

53. This organism would be best classified as:

    A. Endothermic

    B. Halophilic

    C. Thermophilic

    D. Alkaliphilic

54. In the experiment, what is the dependent variable?

    A. Salt concentration

    B. Temperature

    C. Growth rate

    D. Number of snails

55. Which of the following is a trait in humans that undergoes stabilizing selection?

    A. Hair color

    B. Size of head

    C. Blood type

    D. Eye color

56. Dan's pet cat has learned that if she waits at the window when Dan comes home, he will pet her and give her treat. As a result, when he comes home every day, she is waiting at the window. This is an example of:

    A. Instinct

    B. Imprinting

    C. Associative learning

    D. Habit conditioning

57. Which of the following species exhibit phototaxis?

    A. Bears

    B. Salmon

    C. Plants

    D. Moths

58. Dicot plants are distinct from monocot plants because they have two:

    A. Leaves on each branch

    B. Roots

    C. Cotyledons

    D. Pairs of veins in each leaf

59. In which phylum of plantae do ferns belong?

    A. Bryophyte

    B. Tracheophyte

    C. Sporangeophyte

    D. Pterophyte

60. Which of the following is an example of a repressor protein?

    A. Eta operon

    B. Lac operon

    C. TSS site

    D. Distal site

Grid-In Questions

(6 Questions)

1. **Typically, human blood has a pH of 7.2. What is the concentration of hydrogen ions that corresponds to this pH?**

   Answer__________

2. **The current population of Earth is around 7 billion people. If this population continues growing at a rate of 2% annually, how many billion people will be on the Earth in 50 years?**

   Answer__________

3. **The red-haired trait is recessive and not sex-linked. A man has red hair. A woman does not have red hair, but one of her parents had red hair. What is the percent chance that their first child will be a boy and have red hair?**

   Answer__________

4. **A can of soda contains approximately 0.25 mols of glucose. How many mols of ATP will be produced in the human body if all of the glucose is completely used?**

   Answer__________

5. **A scientist notes that if 10 mg of antibiotic is added to a yeast culture, approximately 20% of the cells die every 10 minutes. What proportion of the original yeast cells will remain after 1 hour?**

   Answer__________

6. A florist sees that a recent planting of flowers has 90% red flowers and 10% white flowers. If the red allele is dominant, what is the fraction of the red allele in the population?

Answer_____

Problems 1-2 are long answer. Problems 3-8 are short answer, and should be answered in no more than two short paragraphs.

1. In nature, all living organisms are connected by the food chain, and are thus interdependent. Even though two organisms may not be directly connected in a linear path on the chain, they will interact in some other way due to the population of other species surrounding them. Below is a diagram that shows the interaction of a variety of species found in a lake environment.

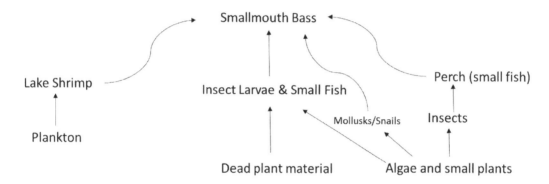

   a. Choose three organisms that exist at different trophic levels in this diagram and explain their inter-relationship and how energy is transferred between each trophic level.

   b. If a toxin were introduced to plants in this system, theorize a potential effect that might occur across the food system.

2. Organisms rely heavily on a variety of proteins to perform essential reactions in their cells and bodies.

   a. Explain the basic steps involved in the expression of a gene.

   b. Not all mutations in a DNA sequence will cause the protein sequence to be changed. Explain how this can be.

   c. Name two factors that can affect the expression of a gene and explain how they either up-regulate or down-regulate the expression pathway.

3. **Mitochondria are unique type of organelles that possess their own set of DNA.**

   a. Describe how mitochondria have their own set of DNA, yet other organelles such as chloroplasts or vacuoles do not.

   b. Mitochondrial DNA is passed to offspring through the mother's side. Explain this phenomenon.

4. **A typical characteristic of a desert biome is that it does not have much organic biomass productivity.**

   a. Using your understanding of a desert environment, explain the lack of biomass productivity in the desert.

   b. Four species that might be found in a desert are the hedgehog cactus, alligator lizard, the plume moth, and the burrowing owl. Describe the relationship on the food chain between these four species, and assign a trophic level to species.

5. **A student plants a garden of tomatoes. The following table shows the production over the first 3 years she has her garden.**

Year	Round Tomatoes	Oval Tomatoes	Wrinkly Tomatoes
1	30	15	5
2	45	11	5
3	50	3	1

Based on this information,

   a. Which allele is dominant and why do you think so?

   b. Propose a possible explanation for the increase of round tomatoes by year three and the corresponding decrease of oval and wrinkly tomatoes.

6. **Phototropic plants will bend toward a source of light. Evolutionarily, this trait is effective for ensuring that plants have access to as much light as possible, improving their chances for survival.**

   a. Describe the process by which a plant can bend its stalk, and at least one of the plant compounds responsible.

   b. Describe the natural selection process that may have enabled some plants to be phototropic.

7. **DNA is the 'code' of human life. Describe the structure of DNA, and explain the process by which one form of DNA mutation can occur.**

8. **The kingdom Monera is a unique kingdom. Name three key traits of species belonging to the kingdom Monera.**

Answer Key

Multiple Choice

1. B	21. C	41. A
2. B	22. A	42. C
3. C	23. C	43. A
4. B	24. B	44. B
5. A	25. A	45. A
6. B	26. D	46. A
7. D	27. D	47. D
8. C	28. A	48. A
9. B	29. B	49. B
10. C	30. B	50. A
11. B	31. A	51. B
12. B	32. C	52. A
13. A	33. C	53. C
14. B	34. B	54. C
15. C	35. A	55. B
16. B	36. C	56. C
17. A	37. D	57. D
18. B	38. B	58. C
19. D	39. A	59. D
20. A	40. C	60. B

Grid-In Questions

1. The pH = -log(H+ concentration). Thus, the concentration is:

   $$10^{-pH} \cdot 10^{-7.2} = 6.3 \times 10^{-8} \text{ M of hydrogen ions.}$$

2. This is a population growth problem, and can be set up as $7 \times (1.02)^{50}$. The basic equation is Future population = present population $\times (1 + \text{rate})^n$, where *n* is number of years. The answer to this question is 18.84 billion. An answer of 18.8 can be accepted.

3. This is a recessive autosomal gene. The man has red hair, meaning both his alleles are recessive. The woman does not have red hair, but one of her parents did. That means she must be heterozygous for the trait. Thus, there is a 50% chance that their children will have red hair.

4. One molecule of glucose can produce 38 ATP's, but will consume 8 ATP in the process. As a result, a net 30 ATP is produced during complete oxidation of glucose. In this case, 0.25 mols of glucose are used. $0.25 \times 30 = 7.5$ mols of ATP produced.

5. If 20% die every 10 minutes, then the equation can be set up as 1×0.8^6 to find out how many cells remain. We find that 0.26 or 26% of cells remain after 1 hour.

6. According to the Hardy-Weinberg equilibrium, roughly double the number of homozygous recessive alleles is present as heterozygous. Thus, given a 10% recessive number, we know that 20% should be heterozygous. This means that the allele fraction is 70% + 10% = 80% of alleles are red.

Free Response

1. The student needs to show an understanding of the different trophic levels.

    a. Three organisms should be chosen, their trophic level named, and the relationship to the level above and below them needs to be described. The description of energy transfer also needs to occur. For example, Bass will eat perch. The transfer of energy occurs through the oxidation of protein and lipids contained in the perch into energy for the bass.

    b. The student should recognize that a toxin introduced at the producer level would affect everything in this food chain. They should explain the link between the producer level, and describe the possible effects as the toxin moves its way up the ladder.

2. The student should:

    a. Explain the steps of expression, including DNA transcription, reading of RNA by a ribosome, creation of an amino acid chain, and subsequent protein folding.

    b. Understand that a codon of 3 nucleotides codes for an amino acid, and that there is more than one 3 nucleotide sequence for each amino acid. As a result, not all mutations cause a change in protein structure.

    c. Explain up-regulation and down-regulation of a gene. This can occur through a promoter sequence or a repressor sequence.

3. The student should show an understanding that the mitochondria were originally their own cells. Since the egg (in humans) is the sex cell that contains mitochondria, the mitochondrial DNA is always only passed on through the mother.

4. The student should be able to explain that:

   a. Biomass productivity is directly related to the amount of biomass created at the producer level. Since the desert is dry and very hot, not much plant biomass is produced, resulting in a net lack of biomass productivity.

   b. These four are at 4 different levels of the food chain, organized as owl -> lizard ->moth -> cactus.

5. The student should recognize that the most common allele is usually the dominant one. In addition, the dominant allele is usually evolutionarily preferred, as can be seen from its increase over time. The student should also be able to explain or theorize that oval or wrinkly tomatoes have some inherent disadvantage (bad seeds, more likely to be eaten by birds) which results in their slow but eventual removal from the genetic pool.

6. The student should be able to:

   a. Explain the basic process of stem elongation, including the hormones auxin and expansin.

   b. Understand that light is vital to the survival of plants, and as a result plants that exhibit phototropism have an advantage over those that do not.

7. The primary points to discuss are:

   a. The four bases of DNA

   b. The helical structure of DNA

   c. The presence of a sugar backbone

   d. One form of DNA mutation such as UV exposure, mis-replication, or chemical exposure

8. Traits of the Kingdom Monera include:

    a. No nucleus

    b. All unicellular

    c. Consist of the majority of bacteria

    d. Reproduce through mitosis

Multiple Choice

1. In a certain town in Middleton, Alabama, a family has had two children, a boy and a girl. What is the percent chance that their next two children will be a boy, and then a girl, in that order?

   A. 25

   B. 33

   C. 50

   D. 75

2. The ozone layer is composed of molecules of O_3, which assist in shielding the Earth from ultraviolet radiation. Ozone can be broken down by chlorofluorocarbons into what product?

   A. Oxygen

   B. OH·

   C. O_2-

   D. Ozone is not broken down by chlorofluorocarbons

3. In the citric acid cycle, how many runs of the cycle are required to process one molecule of glucose?

   A. 1

   B. 2

   C. 3

   D. 4

4. A bacteria has been newly discovered that uses a unique molecule, named by the discovering scientist uberquinone, to transport electrons. Where might this molecule be found?

   A. In the nucleus

   B. In the Golgi body

   C. In the vacuoles

   D. In the mitochondria

5. In fish gills, the extraction of air from water requires that the gills have:

   A. High surface area

   B. High density

   C. High concentration of catalysts

   D. High flexibility

6. A student proposes the idea that the modern day sparrow is a descent of the genus Archaeopteryx, an ancient bird. Which of the following findings would help support this hypothesis?

   A. The finding that Archaeopteryx and sparrows had the same diet.

   B. The finding that Archaeopteryx and sparrows lived in the same region.

   C. The finding that Archaeopteryx and sparrows were both able to fly.

   D. The finding that Archaeopteryx and sparrows share bone structure homology.

7. A halophile is an organism able to withstand:

   A. High temperatures

   B. High concentrations of acid

   C. High concentrations of base

   D. High concentrations of salt

8. **The plant hormone gibberellin is seen in which of the following plant processes?**

    A. Male gamete production

    B. Female gamete production

    C. Root absorption of water

    D. Phototropism

9. **A student designs an experiment in which he needs to collect data on the stem length of a species of tulip in a one-acre field. In order to make sure his samples are unbiased, which of the following influences should he consider before gathering the samples?**

    A. The amount of light that each part of the field receives.

    B. The amount of water that each part of the field receives.

    C. The number of insect pests in the field.

    D. None of the above. Because this is not a comparative experiment, but rather an observational one, there is no need to check for these types of biases.

10. **During the process of aerobic respiration, the movement of which of these ions is responsible for the generation of a large amount of ATP?**

    A. Potassium

    B. Hydrogen

    C. Sodium

    D. Chlorine

11. **Which of the following is the primary distinguishing feature separating C3 from C4 plants?**

    A. C3 plants use the Krebs cycle and C4 plants use the Citric acid cycle.

    B. C3 plants produce a 3-carbon glucose precursor whereas C4 plants produce a 4-carbon glucose precursor.

    C. C4 plants are able to tolerate extreme cold temperatures but C3 plants cannot.

    D. C4 plants produce four molecules of ATP per round of the citric acid cycle whereas C3 plants only produce three molecules of ATP per round of the citric acid cycle.

12. **Which of the following species *cannot* travel across a cell membrane without the use of energy?**

    A. Water

    B. Potassium

    C. Sodium

    D. Glucose

13. **The type of bond responsible for the cohesion of water, the crystallinity of cellulose, and some interactions between amino acids in proteins is:**

    A. Hydrogen bond

    B. Covalent bond

    C. Di-sulfide bond

    D. None of the above

14. **An amino acid contains an "R" functional group, an amino group, and a:**

    A. Hydroxyl group

    B. Carboxyl group

    C. Phenyl group

    D. Phosphate group

15. **Based on the molecular structure of glucose, if a single molecule of glucose is completed consumed by aerobic respiration, how many molecules of carbon dioxide will be formed?**

    A. 3

    B. 6

    C. 9

    D. 12

16. **Prokaryotic organisms are seen in the domain(s):**

    A. Archaea only

    B. Bacteria and Animalia

    C. Animalia and Fungi

    D. Archaea and Bacteria

17. **To increase gene expression what would a repressor protein bind to?**

    A. The operator

    B. The promoter

    C. The intron

    D. The exon

18. In the figure below representing an enzyme, if the square is a substrate, what might the triangle represent?

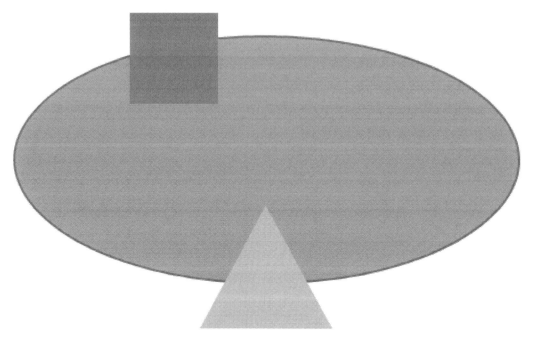

A. An amino acid chain

B. A co-factor

C. A lipid molecule

D. A t-RNA molecule

19. Some bacteria have been found to have Photosystem I, but not II. However, all plants have both PS I and PS II. This implies that:

A. Bacteria evolved from plants, but only received part of the genes for PS I.

B. The genes for PS I are ancestral, and plants are later on the evolution chain.

C. PS I is not able to work in photosynthesis by itself.

D. None of the above.

20. Which of the following would have a large effect on C3 plants, but not on C4 plants?

   A. An increase in atmospheric nitrogen.

   B. An increase in atmospheric oxygen.

   C. An increase in atmosphere carbon dioxide.

   D. An increase in water availability.

21. What color of tinted plastic will protect greenhouse windows from early summer heat while ensuring that the plants still get enough light?

   A. Blue

   B. Red

   C. Green

   D. Yellow

22. A student looks into a microscope and sees a cell that looks like this:

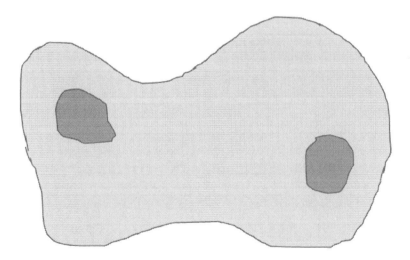

This cell is most likely in:

   A. Prophase

   B. Metaphase

   C. Anaphase

   D. Telophase

23. In mammals, when the egg is released, it is usually accompanied by a body known as the:

A. Placenta

B. Corpus luteum

C. Ovary

D. Follicle

24. Which of the following is the human body's first layer of defense against pathogens?

A. The skin

B. T-cells

C. B-cells

D. Phagocytes

25. A scientist believes that the ostrich and the penguin are related, because of a similar set of bones found in their wings. This relatedness is called:

A. Sympatric speciation

B. Phrenology

C. Homology

D. Pyrodictum

26. The life cycle below is typical of which of the following types of species?

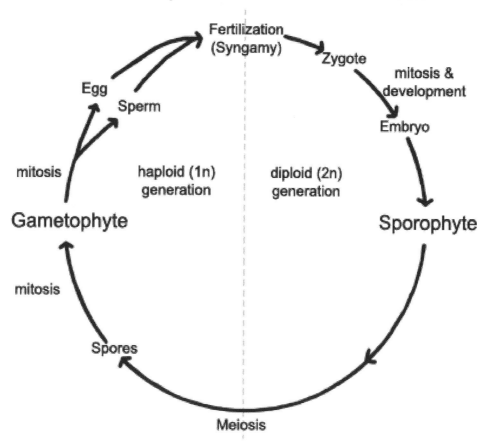

Plant Life Cycle-Alternation of Generation

A. Animals

B. Bacteria

C. Plants and algae

D. Fungi and ferns

27. **A mutation has been introduced into a breed of fruit flies that prevents synapsis from occurring. This will also prevent:**

   A. Histone condensation

   B. Expression of genes

   C. Crossing over

   D. Mitosis

28. **A person examines a fruit fly crossing expected to be 50% red-eyed and 50% white eyed. However, in the offspring, there are 158 red-eyed flies and 189 white-eyed flies. What is the chi-squared value for this data?**

   A. 2.39

   B. 2.45

   C. 2.61

   D. 2.77

29. **The tryptophan operon is a repressible operon. This operon will:**

   A. Turn off whenever tryptophan is present.

   B. Turn on whenever tryptophan is present.

   C. Always be on unless tryptophan is removed.

   D. Always be off without activation by ATP and tryptophan.

30. **Which of the following is not a method by which DNA expression can be controlled?**

   A. Operon

   B. Methylation

   C. Promotion

   D. Sulfonation

31. As global warming occurs, the average temperature of the Earth slowly rises. If this continues, then northern coniferous forests, such as those seen in the northern U.S. and Canada, will eventually be replaced by:

    A. Tropical forest

    B. Desert

    C. Temperate broadleaf forest

    D. Tundra

32. The Allee effect is a term used in population ecology that describes a population which has:

    A. Become so large the environment can no longer sustain it.

    B. Become so small that it will be difficult to survive as a population.

    C. Become so disperse that individuals do not commonly see one another.

    D. Become so dense that it is easy for predators to fix on the population.

33. The carrying capacity of a certain forest is in the range of about 5000 deer. If there are currently 5500 deer in the forest, what will happen?

    A. The extra 500 deer will immediately die.

    B. The number of deer will slowly approach the carrying capacity of 5000.

    C. More predators will appear in order to control the number of deer.

    D. The plants in the forest will eventually evolve to feed more deer.

34. The light reactions in plants occur in which organelle?

    A. Vacuole

    B. Mitochondria

    C. Golgi Body

    D. Chloroplast

35. Which square in the Punnett Square below is filled out incorrectly?

	X	X
X	A Xx	B XX
X	C XX	D XX

A. A

B. B

C. C

D. D

36. Which of the following processes is not seen in the nitrogen cycle?

A. Nitrogen fixation

B. Ammonification

C. Nitrification

D. Amination

37. In the following comparative statements between aerobic respiration and photosynthesis, which statement is true?

   A. Photosynthesis uses less electron flow than aerobic respiration.

   B. Water is produced as part of the photosynthetic process, but not in aerobic respiration.

   C. Carbon dioxide is produced in aerobic respiration, but not in photosynthesis.

   D. Aerobic respiration uses the electron transport chain, whereas photosynthesis does not.

38. Phenylketonuria is a genetic disease in which a person cannot digest phenylalanine. This is due to a lack of a particular:

   A. Gene

   B. Organelle

   C. Organ

   D. Transcription factor

39. If the Hardy-Weinberg equilibrium and its assumptions was absolutely true in all cases, this would result in:

   A. A lack of evolution

   B. A lack of species

   C. A reduction in the survivability of species

   D. An increase in the number of predators vs. producers

40. In the following pathway from A to E, each step is catalyzed by an enzyme. If you wanted to use feedback inhibition to regulate the production of product E, then product E would inhibit the pathway of:

$$A \rightarrow B \rightarrow C \rightarrow D \rightarrow E$$

A. A to B

B. B to D

C. B to C

D. D to E

41. Fungi are organisms that are characterized as:

A. Heterotrophs

B. Autotrophs

C. Symbionts

D. Semi-autotrophs

42. In a nerve impulse, an influx of sodium ions causes the cell potential to rise. What ion is primarily responsible for the restoration of the resting potential afterwards?

A. Calcium

B. Chlorine

C. Potassium

D. Oxygen

43. Which of the followings sets of biomes is organized correctly from least rainfall to most rainfall?

A. Savanna, rainforest, taiga

B. Taiga, grassland, desert

C. Desert, grassland, temperate deciduous forest

D. Tundra, rainforest, coniferous forest

44. A scientist tracks the amount of rainfall in a small town and the corresponding water level in the lake nearby. Based on the data presented in the graph below, which of the following conclusions can be reached?

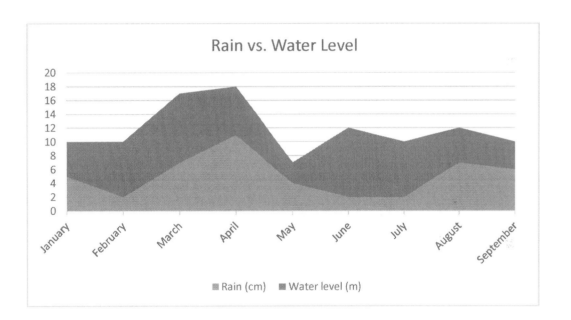

A. The rainfall and water level are strongly correlated.

B. The rainfall and water level are weakly correlated.

C. The rainfall and water level are not correlated at all.

D. The rainfall and water have a negative correlation.

45. Which of the following compounds is not produced by the citric acid cycle?

A. NADH

B. GTP

C. ATP

D. FADH

46. The primary difference between a hydrocarbon and a fatty acid is which of the following structures?

A. $-NH_3$

B. $-COOH$

C. $-OH$

D. $-CH_2OH$

47. A strand of DNA isolated by a scientist has the following sequence:

3'- ATGGTGCTTAGT – 5'

If an mRNA transcript were made, the sequence would be:

A. 5'- TACCACGAATCA -3'

B. 5' –UTCCTCGUUTCA – 3'

C. 5' – UACCAGAAUCA – 3'

D. 5' – GTCAAGTACCA – 3'

48. If a hypotonic cell is removed from its current solution and placed into a solution with 50 mM salt, which of the following will occur?

A. The cell will swell up

B. The cell will shrink

C. The cell will maintain its current volume

D. This question cannot be answered from the information given.

49. The CED genes and caspases are associated with which biological process?

A. G-protein coupled receptors

B. The Krebs Cycle

C. Apoptosis

D. Meiosis

50. In eukaryotic cells, DNA expression is partially regulated by the construction of nucleosomes, which are condensed units of DNA. Nucleosomes are formed through:

A. Binding of histone proteins

B. Binding of methyl and phosphate groups

C. Attachment of DNA condensase

D. Removal of existing DNA polymerase enzymes on the strand of DNA

51. A student is analyzing a compound using mass spectroscopy and finds the following molecular fragments:

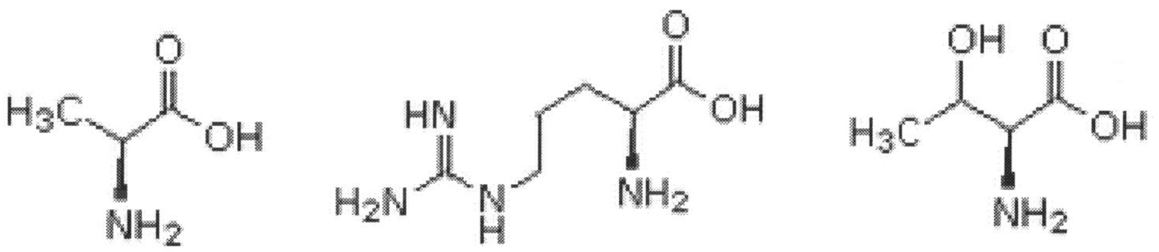

Based on this finding, the compound that was broken down was a:

A. Carbohydrate

B. Protein

C. Lipid

D. Steroid hormone

52. For allopatric speciation to occur, which of the following is necessary?

A. An environmental stress must be introduced

B. A population of a species must be separated into two separate geographic locations

C. A mutagen is put into contact with the species

D. None of the above is necessary. Allopatric speciation occurs slowly and inevitably.

53. In humans, the organ responsible for producing the hormone that regulates blood glucose levels is the:

A. Liver

B. Pancreas

C. Pineal gland

D. Thalamus

54. Ladybugs are pollinators, and they are attracted to the red color of a particular plant's flowers. They pollinate the flowers of the plant, and they mate near the plants. Over time, a new mutant is introduced in the plant population, which has yellow flowers. Some of the ladybugs start to pollinate and mate on the yellow flowers. Eventually, the two subtypes of ladybugs have differentiated and can no longer mate with one another. This is an example of:

A. Allopatric speciation driven by geographic isolation

B. Sympatric speciation driven by behavioral isolation

C. Allopatric speciation driven by natural selection

D. Sympatric speciation driven by habitat differentiation

55. Which two species will share the greatest amount of homology and genes?

A. Those in the same family

B. Those in the same order

C. Those in the same kingdom

D. Those in the same class

Questions 56-58 refer to the following information and table.

A student has designed an experiment to compare the rate of respiration seen in grasshoppers and lizards. She sets up a device known as a respirometer, which is able to measure a change in volume of gas. After performing her experiment, she obtains the following data:

Species	Temp (C)	Respiration Rate (mL O_2 /g /min
Grasshopper	15	0.08134
Grasshopper	30	0.05611
Lizard	15	0.1175
Lizard	30	0.0923

56. Which of the following conclusions can be drawn?

A. As temperature increases, respiration rate increases

B. Lizards are more susceptible to temperature changes than grasshoppers

C. As temperature decreases, respiration rate increases

D. Grasshoppers and lizards' respiration rates are not significantly affected by temperature

223

57. A respirometer measures changes in volume of gas. However, respiration also produces CO_2. In order to make sure that the volume of gas decrease is attributable to only oxygen, which of the following should be done?

   A. A valve should be incorporated that releases excess oxygen in the device.

   B. A substance should be introduced that absorbs CO_2

   C. Oxygen should be added periodically to the device to maintain the volume.

   D. Water vapor should be vented from the device.

58. The student's hypothesis was as follows: Larger animals will have a higher respiration rate due to a higher requirement for energy, which requires O_2 to be consumed. Her hypothesis will be:

   A. Confirmed

   B. Rejected

   C. Rejected due to lack of a proper control

   D. Inconclusive due to lack of data

59. In fermentation, yeast is fed glucose and other sugars, and produces carbon dioxide as a byproduct. Another major byproduct is:

   A. Lactic acid

   B. Pyruvate

   C. Ethanol

   D. Butanol

60. Which of the following is true when comparing large animals to small animals?

A. Large animals have a higher efficiency of respiration than small animals

B. Large animals are more likely to be predators than small animals

C. Large animals have a smaller surface area to volume ratio than small animals

D. Large animals have a slower metabolic rate than small animals

Grid-In Questions

(6 Questions)

1. **A brown seeded pea plant (homozygous gg) was crossed with a green seeded pea plant (heterozygous Gg). The resulting offspring were obtained:**

PHENOTYPE	#
BROWN SEED	67
GREEN SEED	75

Calculate the chi-squared value, rounded to the nearest 100th.

Answer _____

2. **A cell has a diameter of 50 micrometers. Assuming it is perfectly spherical, what is its surface area to volume ratio?**

Answer _____

3. **A population of big-horned sheep was discovered in Yellowstone in the early 1800's. If the population was 120 sheep, and 10 years later, there were 154 sheep, what was the average rate of growth each single year?**

Answer _____

4. **An enzyme has a specific activity rate of 25 s^{-1}. If there is 0.1 mmol of substrate in a 1-liter solution, how many units of enzyme are required to react with all the substrate within 1 hour?**

Answer _____

5. The pH of a solution was found to be 2.5. What is the hydrogen ion concentration in this solution?

   Answer _____

6. A cell has an internal concentration of 100 μmol potassium. If the external concentration is 25 μmol, what will be the equilibrium concentration inside the cell?

   Answer _____

Free Response

Problems 1-2 are long answer. Problems 3-8 are short answer, and should be answered in no more than two short paragraphs.

1. **Photosynthesis will produce sugars in plants. However, the rate at which photosynthesis occurs in a plant is believed to be influenced by several factors. These factors could include the intensity of light available, the temperature of the environment, available water, available carbon dioxide, and even available soil nutrients. If you wanted to test whether one of these variables is important in the rate of photosynthesis, how would you design an experiment to do so?**

    a. Pick a plant and a variable and design an experiment to test the effect of the variable on photosynthesis.

    b. How can the rate of photosynthesis be measured? Will the plants need to be destroyed or can they be kept alive?

    c. State a hypothesis, and what results (or lack of results) would need to be seen in order to prove the hypothesis.

2. **The graph below represents the amount of rainfall a semi-arid desert region has received over the past 100 years.**

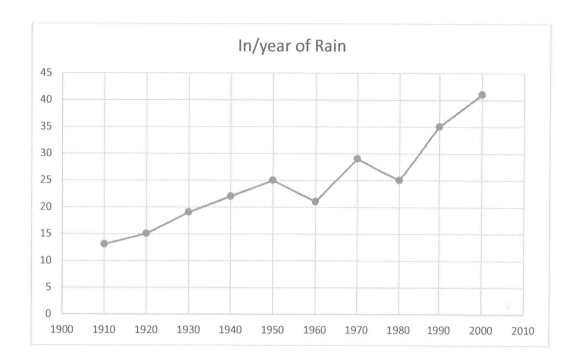

a. Based on this data, provide a description of how this biome might look like in the year 2020.

b. What would be the best categorization of this biome in the year 2000? Explain your justification.

c. Assuming that the trend seen in the graph continues, what will happen to the species currently living in this biome?

3. **Cell communication is an important facet of day-to-day life. Explain one form of communication that can occur between human immune system cells, and why it is crucial to the entire organism.**

4. Homeostasis is an important set of regulatory mechanisms that exist in all species in order to attempt to maintain a set of conditions beneficial to the organism. Choose two of the following regulatory mechanisms and explain their function and use.

   a. Water balance in plant cells.

   b. Body temperature in mammals.

   c. Glucose concentration in blood.

   d. Calcium concentration in muscle tissue.

5. In many species, RNA is transcribed from DNA, and then expressed in the form of a protein. However, retroviruses only contain RNA. Explain the basic process through which RNA can be converted to DNA, and the life cycle of a retrovirus.

6. John is brown-haired and blue-eyed. Anne is blonde-haired and brown-eyed. Brown hair is a dominant gene, with B representing the dominant allele and b representing the recessive allele, which results in blonde hair. Brown eyes are a dominant gene, and with R representing the dominant allele and r representing the recessive allele, which results in blue eyes. Draw a Punnett Square that represents the gene possibilities if John and Anne have children. Both parents are homozygous in both alleles.

7. A population of ants lives next to a river. One day, half of the population travels across the river, to a new environment, and sets up a colony there. Which type of evolution might occur, and why?

8. Explain in brief the function and use of histones with regard to DNA regulation.

Answer Key

Multiple Choice

1.	A	21.	A	41.	A
2.	A	22.	D	42.	C
3.	C	23.	B	43.	C
4.	D	24.	A	44.	B
5.	A	25.	C	45.	D
6.	D	26.	C	46.	B
7.	D	27.	C	47.	C
8.	D	28.	D	48.	D
9.	D	29.	A	49.	C
10.	B	30.	D	50.	A
11.	B	31.	C	51.	B
12.	D	32.	B	52.	B
13.	A	33.	B	53.	B
14.	B	34.	D	54.	D
15.	B	35.	C	55.	A
16.	D	36.	D	56.	C
17.	A	37.	C	57.	B
18.	B	38.	A	58.	A
19.	B	39.	A	59.	C
20.	C	40.	A	60.	C

1. The answer is 0.45. The solution is calculated using the chi-square formula, which is:

$$ X^2 = \sum \frac{(\text{Observed Value} - \text{Expected Value})^2}{(\text{Expected Value})} $$

2. The answer is 0.12. The solution is calculated by using the formulas for surface area ($A = 4\pi r^2$) and volume ($V = 4/3 * \pi r^3$) for a sphere. Then divide the surface area by the volume.

3. The answer is 0.025, or 2.5%. Set up the population growth equation: $P = P0*(1+\text{rate})^n$. P is given as 154, and P0 is 120. n is 10 years. Thus:

$$ 154 = 120*(1+x)^{10} $$

$$ 1.283 = (1+x)^{10} $$

$$ \ln(1.283) = 10*\ln(1+x) $$

$$ 0.249/10 = \ln(1+x) $$

$$ 0.0249 = \ln(1+x) $$

Using some guess and check at this point, we can find that x = 0.025, or 2.5%.

4. The answer is 6.7×10^{15}. There is 1 mmol in 1 liter, or 1 mmol total, which is 6.022×10^{20} molecules. We take that and divide it by 3600 seconds (1 hour), and 25 units per second to find the answer.

5. The answer is 0.003 molar. The pH = -log(H+). The (H+) = 10^{-pH}.

6. The answer is 25 μmol. This is a trick question, and references the flow of potassium into and out of a cell during a nerve impulse. The environment is much larger than the cell itself. Thus, at equilibrium, the cell concentration will always equal the original environmental concentration.

1. The student picks a plant and a variable to test (for example, water.) We will assume that since plants are autotrophs, the rate of photosynthesis can be directly correlated to the mass of the plant. Thus, we can test this by designing an experiment in which the amount of water is varied (for example, 100 mL/day, 200 mL/day, etc.), and the mass of the plant is measured. Through this method, the plant can be kept alive. If the student says the plants must be killed, they should provide an adequate justification of why. An example hypothesis: Based on the need for water to provide hydrogen and oxygen into the photosynthetic process, an increased amount of water should increase the rate of photosynthesis.

2. The graph clearly shows an average increase in rainfall in this biome. This means that in the year 2000, the biome is no longer desert, which receives less than 15 in/year of rain. It is more likely now a grassland or savanna region. From this trend, we can assume that the species living in the region in 1910 will have moved or adapted. New species will have entered the area due to more plants growing and more water being available.

3. Examples include: B cell signaling, Phagocytes swarming to T-cells, etc. Another example is Helper T-cells that produce cytokines, which activate immune responses, telling other cells to come to the antigen or wound.

4. For the four options:

   a. Water balance needs to be explained from the roots to the leaves. Tonicity needs to be mentioned, as well as transpiration.

   b. Body temperature regulation is maintained by features with large surface areas, such as the ears or hands.

   c. Glucose concentration in blood is regulated by the pancreas and insulin. There needs to be a description of insulin function as well as glycogen and storage of sugar.

   d. Calcium concentration is regulated by calcium pumps, which use ATP. Calcium is required for muscle action.

5. The student should explain the process of RNA reverse transcriptase and how it converts RNA to DNA. The life cycle of a virus should also be explained, from initial injection of DNA/RNA, then the use of the cell's machinery to create more viruses, and then the lysing of the host cell.

6. John is BBrr, and Anne is bbRR. The Punnett Square should be:

	Br	Br	Br	Br
bR	BbRr	BbRr	BbRr	BbRr
bR	BbRr	BbRr	BbRr	BbRr
bR	BbRr	BbRr	BbRr	BbRr
bR	BbRr	BbRr	BbRr	BbRr

All of their children will have the same genotype and phenotype, with brown hair and brown eyes.

7. This is an example of allopatric speciation, because the two populations are now geographically separated. Depending on the conditions in the new environment, several different types of speciation might occur, including behavioral, temporal, or some other environmental factor based.

8. Histones are proteins that are used to wrap around and condense DNA. DNA in its native state is very long, and in order to be condensed into chromatids and then chromosomes, histones are needed to perform the condensation.

Multiple Choice

1. **Water is an important molecule for life, due to all of the following properties, except for:**

    A. It has a high heat capacity.

    B. It is a good solvent for many different molecules and chemicals

    C. It has a high surface tension and cohesion

    D. It is a necessary ingredient in the formation of many elements

2. **In the Miller-Urey experiment, which attempted to replicate conditions that were existent in early Earth, which of the following compounds was *not* created?**

    A. Amino acids

    B. Methane

    C. Lipid precursors

    D. Chlorophyll

3. **Which of the following will occur if more cis-bonds are added between the carbons in a long chain fatty acid?**

    A. The temperature at which the fatty acid will become solid will increase.

    B. The temperature at which the fatty acid will become solid will decrease.

    C. The solubility of the fatty acid in hexane will increase.

    D. The solubility of the fatty acid in hexane will decrease.

4. **Although plant cells and animal cells are roughly the same size, the volume of cytosol, or plasma, inside an animal cell is significantly larger than that seen in a plant cell. What is responsible for this difference?**

    A. The presence of chlorophyll in plant cells.

    B. The presence of an endoplasmic reticulum in plant cells.

    C. The presence of a large storage vacuole in plant cells.

    D. The presence of a cell wall in plant cells.

5. **Richard has a theory that the color of light a plant receives will change the rate of growth of that plant. He sets up an experiment to test this idea. One group of plants is exposed to green light, and the other is given blue light. What third group of plants should be tested in this experiment?**

    A. A group of plants not exposed to light.

    B. A group of plants given excess water.

    C. A group of plants exposed to white light.

    D. A group of plants first exposed to green light, and then to blue light.

6. **Chaperone molecules are used to aid in the formation of:**

    A. A protein's amino acid chain

    B. A protein's tertiary structure

    C. A mRNA repeating tail end

    D. The mRNA-ribosome complex

7. **In the process of aerobic respiration, which of the following occurs?**

    A. The lysis of glucose

    B. The oxidation of glucose

    C. The synthesis of glucose

    D. The transformation of glucose

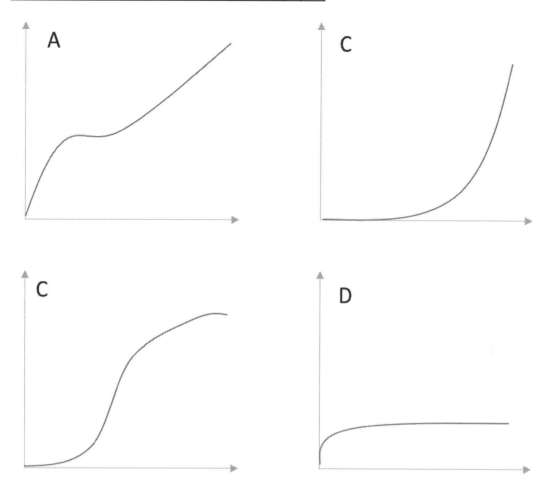

8. **Which of the following statements best describes graph C?**

    A. A bacterial culture with the presence of antibiotics

    B. A mixotrophic bacterial culture

    C. A bacterial culture with unlimited nutrients

    D. A bacterial culture containing a virus

9. Tom is growing a yeast culture. He places yeast onto an agar plate and allows it to grow. He tracks the number of cells over a one-week time frame. The graph of cells vs. time will most likely resemble:

    A. Graph A

    B. Graph B

    C. Graph C

    D. Graph D

10. Viruses are composed of a capsid shell made of various proteins and sugars. The capsid properties are important in determining the viruses' infectiousness and survivability. Among the other facts listed below about viruses, which of the following is *not* true?

    A. A nucleophyte is a viral precursor that only contains a small fragment of DNA.

    B. Some animal viruses are able to enter host cells through the process of endocytosis.

    C. Some viruses contain RNA instead of DNA inside their capsid.

    D. Bacteriophages inject DNA directly into their host cell, leaving behind their capsid.

11. In the skeletal muscle action potential, seen below, what is responsible for the increase of membrane potential?

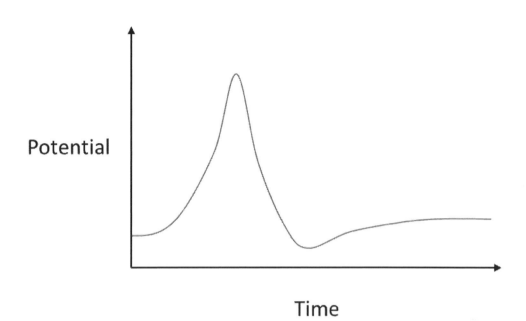

A. Influx of Na only

B. Influx of Na and K

C. Influx of Na and Ca

D. Influx of Ca and K

12. Which of the following is the primary difference between pyrimidines and purines?

A. A pyrimidine has two amino groups and a purine has only one.

B. A purine has two carbon-nitrogen rings and a pyrimidine has only one.

C. Pyrimidines are found in DNA and purines are found in RNA.

D. Purines are aromatic compounds and Pyrimidines are not.

13. Which of the following statements about the electron transport chain is true?

   A. Molecules called plastoquinones are involved in transporting electrons.

   B. The electron transport chain is found in the endoplasmic reticulum and the mitochondria.

   C. The ATP generated from glucose is used to drive electrons across the membrane barrier to produce energy for more ATP.

   D. The electron transport chain receives some electrons from HPO_4.

14. Concerning the cell membrane, the fluid mosaic model proposed that:

   A. The membrane is a fluid object composed of interlocking lipids.

   B. The membrane is a fluid object that contains various proteins and sugars.

   C. The membrane is a amphipathic double layer.

   D. The membrane is able to absorb fluids easily and form them into patterns.

15. A molecule of ATP is formed from a phosphate tail, an adenine head, and a:

   A. Oxaloacetate group

   B. Pyruvate group

   C. Glucose group

   D. Ribose group

16. **Which of the following statements is correct about the reaction described below?**

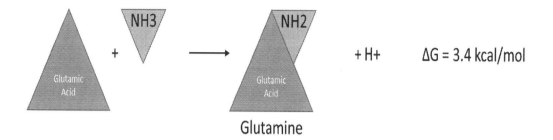

Glutamine

A. The reaction requires a catalyst.

B. The reaction is exothermic.

C. The reaction is endothermic.

D. The reaction has a very fast rate.

17. **Which of the following is not a fermentation product or intermediate?**

A. Lactic acid

B. Ethanol

C. Pyruvate

D. Methanol

18. **In some species, the end of the electron transport chain uses sulfur as an electron acceptor instead of oxygen. Oxygen forms carbon dioxide in aerobic respiration. What does sulfur form?**

A. SO_4

B. HS

C. H_2SO_3

D. HCOS

19. In the citric acid cycle, which molecule needs to be regenerated after each pyruvate is processed?

    A. Ketoglutarate

    B. Oxaloacetate

    C. GADH

    D. Fumarate

20. A sex-linked trait primarily seen in males but sometimes seen in females is passed along in the:

    A. 22nd chromosome

    B. 18th chromosome

    C. X chromosome

    D. Y chromosome

21. In metaphase, the chromosomes become aligned near the center of the cell, and are attached to the centrioles through the:

    A. Chromatin

    B. Kinetochore microtubules

    C. Myosin microtubules

    D. Histones

22. A brown mouse (BB) is mated with a white mouse (bb), where the brown gene color allele is dominant. The offspring will be:

    A. 100% brown

    B. 75% brown

    C. 50% brown

    D. 100% white

23. Where are Okazaki fragments seen?

    A. In DNA replication in the 5' to 3' strand.

    B. In DNA replication in the 3' to 5' strand.

    C. In RNA transcription in the 3' to 5' strand.

    D. In RNA transcription in the 5' to 3' strand.

Questions 24 – 25 are based on the following passage and chart.

A student designs an experiment to test the genetics of the roses seen in his front yard. He mates a red rose with another red rose and produces the F1 generation of offspring. He then randomly selects two of the F1 generation and mates them, resulting in the F2 generation. The results are seen below:

Parent Generation

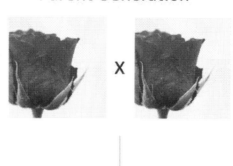

X

F1 generation  100% red roses

F2 generation

75% red roses   25% white roses

24. From this data, it can be concluded that the parent generation had:

    A. Two homozygous parents

    B. Two heterozygous parents

    C. One homozygous and one heterozygous parent

    D. There is not information to reach any conclusion

25. If instead of white roses, the F1 and F2 generation both showed pink roses, it could be that the gene for rose color is:

    A. Heterochromatic

    B. Incompletely dominant

    C. Pleotropic

    D. Randomly non-assorting

26. A student is experimenting with some DNA. He finds that if he removes one small part of the DNA, which is known to code for a protein, the protein does not form at all. The part he removed was likely:

    A. Responsible for a disulfide linkage

    B. The start codon

    C. The promoter sequence

    D. The ribosomal coding sequence

27. In the Crassulacean acid metabolism scheme (CAM) in plants, carbon dioxide is collected during the night and formed into:

    A. Malate

    B. Ribulose

    C. Bisphosphate

    D. Carboxylic acid

28. **A student is investigating the digestion of lactose by a certain bacteria. She notes that lactose is degraded by the enzyme lactase. She also notices that lactase is only produced when lactose is present. The lactase gene is likely controlled by a:**

    A. Negative inducible operon

    B. Positive inducible operon

    C. Negative repressible operon

    D. Positive repressible operon

29. **Charles Darwin based his theory of natural selection on a number of logical observations and premises. Which of the following is *not* one of them?**

    A. Organisms have many more offspring that the environment could be expected to support.

    B. Many species are able to mutate or alter their genes in order to adapt to the environment.

    C. Organisms are unique, and their offspring inherit traits from their parents.

    D. In a given environment, populations of species typically remain about the same throughout time.

30. **An example of modern day evolution is the investigation of a change in moth color after the Industrial revolution began. The burning of coal during this time created a layer of dark soot that appeared on trees, buildings, and grasses. During this time, the color of moths changed from light white or brown to dark gray or black. Which of the following statements about this situation is true?**

    A. The moths changed their color after more soot began appearing.

    B. Prior to the industrial revolution, some moths were already dark gray or black.

    C. The pollution caused by the industrial revolution simply colored the moths black.

    D. The moths became darker in order to blend in.

31. The idea that all modern day species are descended from a single common ancestor is known as the:

    A. Theory of common descent

    B. Mixed gene inheritance theory

    C. Theory of independent assortment

    D. Darwin's First Law

32. A student is working with a population of monkeys. It is expected that ¼ of the monkeys in this generation should have black fur, and the remainder should have brown fur. He finds that there are 8 monkeys with black fur, and 41 with brown fur. What is the chi square value for this data?

    A. 1.76

    B. 1.96

    C. 2.22

    D. 13.45

33. According to the Hardy Weinberg Equilibrium Theory, which of the following statements should be true?

    A. The phenotype variance in a population should stay roughly the same.

    B. The genotype variance in a population should stay roughly the same.

    C. The population size in an area should stay roughly the same.

    D. The allelic frequency of a population is not subject to natural selection pressures.

34. The primary producers in a small lake ecosystem are algae. Robert measured one month that 2085 kg of algae were produced in the lake and consumed by a species of bluegill fish. If the fish *only* consumed the algae, what is a reasonable amount of fish mass produced?

    A. 20.85 kg

    B. 208.5 kg

    C. 417 kg

    D. 505 kg

35. The majority of species are heterotrophs, and rely on autotrophic organisms to produce food that they consume. The food that autotrophs produce stems from energy produced by:

    A. Fission of water

    B. The sun

    C. Geothermal heat

    D. Wind energy

36. The cuticle on a plant is a thin, waxy layer found on the leaves intended to prevent:

    A. Excess evaporation

    B. Consumption by birds

    C. Loss of carbon dioxide from the leaf

    D. Loss of oxygen from the leaf

37. The figure below represents chlorophyll A. What is the purpose of the magnesium atom in the center?

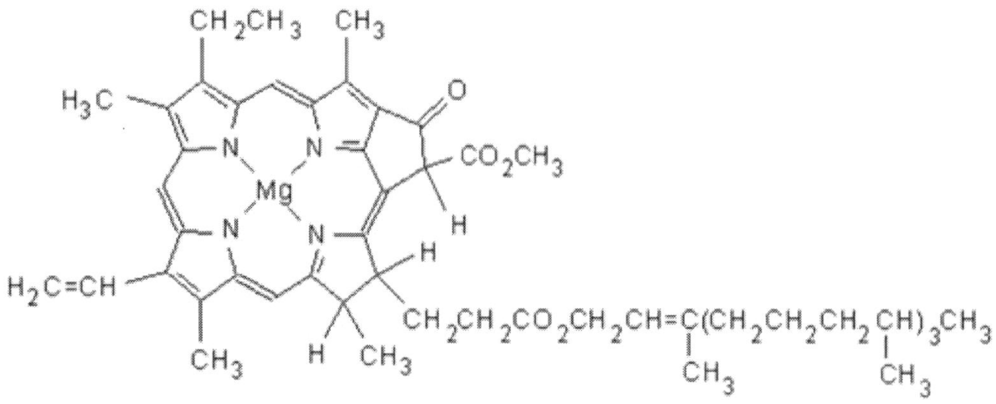

A. The Mg atom's charge increases the stability of the chlorophyll molecule.

B. The Mg complex, when struck by light, excites and releases an electron.

C. The Mg atom stabilizes the intermediate in the splitting of a water molecule.

D. None of the above is correct.

38. The equation below represents the general simplified equation for production of organic material from photosynthesis. What is the correct equation for the formation of glucose from photosynthesis?

$$CO2 + H2O \rightarrow CH2O + O2$$

A. 3 CO2 + 8 H2O → C3H8O6 + 3 O2 + 6 H2O

B. 6 CO2 + 12 H2O → C6H12O6 +6 O2 + 6 H2O

C. 6 CO2 + 12 H2O → 2 C3H6O3 +6 O2 + 6 H2O

D. 3 CO2 + 3 H2O → C4H8O3 + 2 O2 + 2 H2O

39. In plants, light reactions take light energy from the sun to generate:

    A. Glucose and ATP

    B. NADH and Pyruvate

    C. Acetic acid

    D. ATP and NADH

40. Below are four statements regarding mutations. Which of these statements are true?

I. Mutations are always harmful to the individual or species.

II. Mutations can be beneficial.

III. Mutations can occur randomly, without the aid of radiation or chemicals.

IV. Mutations are very infrequent, and happen less than 1% of individuals.

    A. I and II are true.

    B. Only II is true.

    C. II, and III are true.

    D. II, III, and IV are true.

41. Which of the following is not a type of cell connection or junction between cells?

    A. Tight junction

    B. Gap junction

    C. Desmosome

    D. Channel junction

42. The endoplasmic reticulum is broken up into the rough ER and the smooth ER. The rough ER is responsible for synthesis of proteins and some polysaccharides. What is the smooth ER responsible for?

    A. Metabolism of carbohydrates and synthesis of lipids

    B. DNA replication and transcription

    C. Modification of RNA after the transcription process

    D. Degradation of residual amino acids and cell waste products

43. Which of the following is an example of convergent evolution?

    A. The evolution of tails in both whales and sharks

    B. The evolution of pine cones in both southern pine and spruce trees

    C. The evolution of pincers in both ants and termites

    D. The evolution of feathers in both the sparrow and finch

44. Based on the Punnett Square seen below, which of the following *must* be true?

AA	Aa
Aa	aa

A. Only one parent is heterozygous

B. At least one parent is homozygous

C. Both parents are heterozygous

D. Both parents are homozygous

45. A student conducts an experiment measuring the rate of oxygen production by a certain plant. He notices that the rate of oxygen production is rather low during the day, but increases at night. This type of plant is best classified as a:

    A. C3 plant

    B. C4 plant

    C. CAM plant

    D. B2 plant

46. Which of these species subtypes contain silica in their cell wall?

    A. Plants

    B. Red algae

    C. Fungi

    D. Diatoms

47. Which of the following is *not* a non-steroid hormone?

    A. Epinephrine

    B. Dopamine

    C. Estrogen

    D. Oxytocin

48. Compared to neurotransmitters and non-steroid hormones, which act in the order of milliseconds, the response caused by steroid hormones is usually much longer, in terms of hours or even days. What causes this difference?

   A. Steroid hormones act through a multi-step signaling pathway, which takes more time.

   B. Steroid hormones are present in the body at much lower concentrations compared to neurotransmitters.

   C. Steroid hormones are unable to enter the cell membrane through receptors or diffusion.

   D. Steroid hormones turn genes on or off, and the effects of gene products take longer to be seen.

49. In a commensalistic relationship between species, which of the following is true?

   A. Both species gain a communal benefit from interacting with one another.

   B. Only one species gains a benefit from the interaction, but the other species is not harmed.

   C. Both species co-exist peacefully, with neither gaining a positive benefit.

   D. One species gains a benefit from the interaction, at the other species loss.

50. Which of the following scenarios is the most likely to result in a bottleneck effect?

   A. A population of lions is split up into different geographically separate regions.

   B. A pesticide kills 95% of a population of beetles.

   C. Because of a mutation, the gene encoding for chitin in a fungus was disrupted.

   D. The development of a new housing area pushes a species of bird out of the area.

Questions 51-53 are based on the table and information below:

A student is conducting an experiment on the rate of methane production by methanogenic bacteria. He is using a bacteria called *Methanosarcina barkeri*. The bacteria produces methane by the following reaction:

$$CO_2 + 4\ H_2 \rightarrow CH_4 + 2\ H_2O$$

The bacteria live by digesting waste biomass in swamps and bonds, and receive hydrogen from a synergistic organism. The data gathered is below:

Temperature	**Biomass in H2O (g/L)**	**CH4 production (mL/hr)**
15 C	5	1.4
15 C	10	1.8
25 C	5	1.9
25 C	10	2.5

51. Based on this data, which of the following statements is correct?

A. Temperature increases the rate of methane formation

B. Biomass concentration increases the rate of methane formation

C. Hydrogen concentration increases the rate of methane formation

D. None of the above is correct

52. If the student wanted to test the effect of hydrogen concentration in this experiment, which of the following experiments would he *not* need to do?

A. Test the methane production rate at 15 C, 5g/L biomass, and 5 g/L hydrogen.

B. Test the methane production rate at 20 C, 15g/L biomass, and 10g/L hydrogen.

C. Set up a control experiment for each of the three variables.

D. He would need to perform all of the above.

53. *If* it is true that the rate of methane production increased with temperature, then which of the following is also likely true?

    A. The reaction forming methane is endothermic.

    B. The reaction forming methane is exothermic.

    C. The reaction forming methane is catalyzed by biomass in the water.

    D. The reaction forming methane is isothermic.

54. A cell is missing the enzyme DNA helicase. Which of the following will occur?

    A. DNA replication will occur, but the formed DNA will have many mutations.

    B. DNA replication will occur, but the two formed strands of DNA will not be bonded together.

    C. DNA replication will start, but only the 3'->5' end of DNA will be replicated.

    D. DNA replication will not start at all.

55. Most human cells have a concentration of about 5.4% w/v of solutes over solution. If placed into ocean water, which has about 3.5% w/v salt concentration, what will happen?

    A. The human cell will shrink

    B. The human cell will swell

    C. There will be no change in the size of the cell

    D. The cell will start pumping out water

56. In a tree, water is carried from the roots to the top of tree through which type of cells?

    A. Pith

    B. Xylem

    C. Phloem

    D. Schleral cells

57. Which of the following is not true about meristems in plants?

    A. A plant shoot has an apical meristem

    B. A plant root has a root meristem

    C. Damaging a meristem will result in a leaf, flower, or root not forming

    D. In the majority of plants, a single meristem is responsible for the production of flowers

58. The majority of plants grow away from gravity, such that if you invert a potted plant, the stem will curve back, resulting in the plant still facing the sky. This phenomenon is called:

    A. Phototropism

    B. Geotropism

    C. Thermotropism

    D. Chemotropism

59. In the Calvin cycle, the production of a single molecule of glyceraldehyde-3-phosphate requires:

    A. 3 ATP and 3 NADPH

    B. 3 ATP and 6 NADPH

    C. 6 ATP and 6 NADPH

    D. 9 ATP and 6 NADPH

60. **Ashley is travelling abroad, and is investigating a biome characterized by very cold temperatures, sparse grass and trees, and moderate rain and snowfall. This biome is:**

    A. A northern coniferous forest

    B. A tundra

    C. A taiga

    D. A semi-arid steppe

(6 Questions)

1. A student mixes a 1 liter 1M solution of NaOH with a 0.5 liter 3M solution of Na_2PO_4. Assuming complete solvation, what is the concentration of Na^+ ion in the final mixture? Round to the nearest 100th.

   Answer _____

2. A pea plant with the gene alleles Pp is bred with a pea plant with the gene alleles pp. What proportion of the offspring will have the gene alleles Pp?

   Answer _____

3. A scientist finds that the number of turtles with albinism (a recessive bb gene for color) on an island is 24. If 102 other turtles on the island are not albino and 54 of them are homozygous, what is the frequency of the dominant allele?

   Answer _____

4. Overpopulation of deer in an area can be a serious concern for farmers due to crop damage. The deer population in an area is given by:

$$P = P0(1.07)^n - n(2x)$$

   Where P is the population, P0 is the initial population, n is the number of years, and x is the number of deer hunted each year.

   If the initial population is 2300, how many deer need to be hunted each year to make sure the population is less than 2500 in 10 years?

   Answer _____

5. The half-life of titanium-44 is about 63 years. How many half-lives are needed before a 100g sample is reduced to less than 1g?

Answer _____

6. A "small" lake has a volume of 2 cubic kilometers, or 2 x 10^{12} liters. Over a period of 10 years, the pH changed from 7.3 to 7.2. What mass of hydrogen ions in kilograms would need to be added to this lake for this change to occur?

Answer _____

Free Response Questions

Problems 1-2 are long answer. Problems 3-8 are short answer, and should be answered in no more than two short paragraphs.

1. **Suppose there is a population of leopards living in a forest with no natural predators. Propose a scenario in which natural selection of the leopards would occur.**

    a. Distinguish between a genetic drift event and natural selection.

    b. State a possible way the leopard could adapt to the scenario.

    c. If a scientist wanted to prove that the scenario is the cause of evolution in the population of leopards, how would he or she do it?

2. **In a cell, a molecule of mRNA has been recently transcribed from a strand of DNA.**

    a. Before it can be used, what, if any, modifications need to be performed?

    b. How many times can a strand of mRNA be read before translation stops?

    c. Describe the general pathway from mRNA to protein.

3. **Restriction enzymes can be used to cut DNA into fragments based on a 4-5 base pair identification region. Describe how restriction enzymes can be used to detect the presence of a gene.**

4. Below is a representation of a series of genes on a chromosome:

Gene A	Gene B	Gene C	Gene D

Describe the process of crossing over and state which pair of genes will be the most likely to cross over and which pair will be the least likely to cross over.

5. Explain the concept of carrying capacity and give at least two factors in an environment that will affect the carrying capacity.

6. The nervous system works by sending electric pulses along nerve fibers. On the basis of a single cell, describe the generation of this electrical signal and the ions involved.

7. The graph below shows the dissolved oxygen in mg/L on the Y-axis of a lake over a period of 100 years.

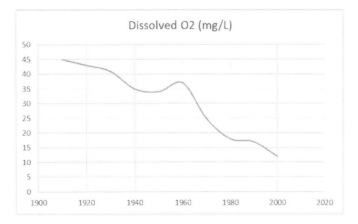

Based on this graph, what is the trophic state of the lake in the year 2000 and why? Propose a reason for the decline of the dissolved O_2 content in the lake.

8. Pattern baldness is a male sex-linked trait. If a man is bald, but his wife is not, what is the percent chance that a daughter from the two parents will be bald? Explain.

Answer Key

Multiple Choice

1. D	21. B	41. C
2. D	22. A	42. D
3. B	23. B	43. A
4. C	24. C	44. A
5. C	25. B	45. C
6. B	26. B	46. C
7. B	27. A	47. D
8. B	28. A	48. C
9. C	29. B	49. D
10. A	30. B	50. B
11. C	31. A	51. D
12. B	32. B	52. B
13. A	33. B	53. A
14. B	34. B	54. D
15. D	35. B	55. B
16. C	36. A	56. B
17. D	37. B	57. D
18. B	38. B	58. B
19. B	39. D	59. D
20. C	40. D	60. B

1. The answer is 2.67 molarity. We calculate the concentration of sodium ions inside the solution. There is 1 liter of a 1M NaOH solution, for 1 mol of Na. There is 0.5 liters of a 3 M Na_2PO_4 solution, which releases two sodium ions per molecule, for a total of 3 mols. The final volume is 1.5 liters. 4 mols / 1.5 liters = 2.67 molarity.

2. The answer is 50%. The Punnett square will look like:

	P	p
p	Pp	pp
p	Pp	pp

As can be seen, half of the plants will have the genotype Pp.

3. The answer is 0.61. The HW equation is $A^2 + 2AB + B^2 = 1$, where A is the dominant allele and B is the recessive allele. There are 136 turtles, for a total of 272 alleles – remember, most species are diploid. We know the frequency of the homozygous recessive (24 turtles = 48 alleles), or 0.176.

- The frequency of the homozygous dominant allele is 108, or 0.397

- Thus, the frequency of the heterozygous alleles is 0.427.

- The frequency of the dominant allele is 0.397 + ½ (0.427), or 0.6105, rounded to 0.61.

4. The answer is 102 deer. The population of the deer after 10 years *without hunting* is P = 2300(1.07)^{10}, or 4524 deer. We need there to be less than 2500 deer, so hunting has to eliminate 2024 deer.

From the equation, we can set it up to be 10*(2x) = 2024. X is solved as 101.2 deer need to be hunted each year. However, we have to have *less* than 2500, so we cannot round down. The correct answer is thus 102 deer.

5. The answer is seven. You don't need to know the half-life length, actually. Each half-life reduces the amount by ½.

Number of half-lives elapsed	Fraction remaining	Percentage remaining
0	$\frac{1}{1}$	100
1	$\frac{1}{2}$	50
2	$\frac{1}{4}$	25
3	$\frac{1}{8}$	12.5
4	$\frac{1}{16}$	6.25
5	$\frac{1}{32}$	3.125
6	$\frac{1}{64}$	1.563
7	$\frac{1}{128}$	0.781
...	...	...
n	$\frac{1}{2^n}$	$100/(2^n)$

6. The answer is 25.95 kilograms of H+ ions. First, calculate change in molarity. pH 7.3 = 5.01×10^{-8} M. pH 7.2 = 6.3×10^{-8} M. The difference is 1.29×10^{-8} M.

   Then calculate the weight needed. The volume is 2×10^{12} liters. 2×10^{12} * 1.29×10^{-8} = 25954 mols. Each mol of hydrogen only weighs 1 g. 25954/1000 = 25.95 kilograms of H+ ions added.

1. The student needs to clearly distinguish between genetic drift, where due to random population sampling, the gene allele frequencies change, and natural selection, where an environmental pressure causes a selection that changes the allele frequency in the population.

   The scenario proposed should involve an environmental pressure, such as a change in food supply or an addition of a predator. Also possible would be a change in temperature or water availability.

   Finally, the student should design an experiment in which random sampling occurs, the scientist has a baseline (before drift or natural selection), and some method for data collection that would show the change in genotype or phenotype of the leopards.

2. The student should review the general process of RNA translation. Before mRNA can be used by a ribosome, it needs to be cut and re-arranged by a spliceosome to remove the intron segments from the code.

   The number of times a piece of mRNA can be translated is regulated by the poly-adenine tail. The student needs to discuss the formation of the tail and what happens once the tail is depleted. Each translation of the mRNA shortens the tail.

3. A restriction enzyme will cut at certain locations. If the gene sequence is known, then the lengths of DNA that will be produced by the cutting of the restriction enzyme will be known. As a result, running the cut product through a gel electrophoresis will show a certain band pattern.

4. Genes are less likely to cross over the closer they are together. The student should state that that genes B and C are the least likely to cross over. They should state that crossing over occurs in Meiosis I (not Meiosis II!) and describe the general process.

5. A carrying capacity is the capacity of an environment in terms of resources to support a population of a species. Factors include available biomass from autotrophs (grasses, trees, etc.), water, number of predators, etc.

6. The generation of a nerve potential should include:

   - Influx of Na+ ions to increase cell potential

   - Restoration of resting potential by K+

   - Travel of the electrical signal through the nerve fiber dendrites and axons.

7. The trophic state can be determined by the amount of dissolved oxygen. A lake with a high amount of dissolved oxygen is classified as oligotrophic or mesotrophic. A lake with a low amount of dissolved oxygen is eutrophic and has too many nutrients that are enabling bacteria and small organisms to thrive and reduce the oxygen levels.

8. A male sex-linked trait is passed along in the X chromosome. The student should state that a man's sex chromosomes are XY and a woman's are XX. They should further state that if the woman is heterozygous for the trait, there is a 50% chance a daughter will have pattern-baldness. If the woman is homozygous dominant, then there is a 0% chance the daughter will have pattern baldness.

Image Sources

1. Periodic Table
   http://www.wpclipart.com/science/atoms_molecules/periodic_tables/periodic_table_of_elements_BW.png.html

2. Hydrogen Bond Picture - Original

3. Lipid Picture - Adapted from:
   http://en.wikipedia.org/wiki/File:Common_lipids_lmaps.png

4. Histidine Molecule - Original

5. Phospholipid Molecule Structure - Adapted from:
   http://en.wikipedia.org/wiki/File:Membrane_lipids.png

6. Cell membrane bilayer - Original

7. Tonicity Figure, water entering cell - Original

8. Cellular metabolism figure - Original

9. ATP Molecule
   http://en.wikipedia.org/wiki/File:Adenosintriphosphat_protoniert.svg

10. Ethanol Fermentation - Original

11. Leaf structure – Adapted from:
    http://commons.wikimedia.org/wiki/File:Leaf_anatomy_universal.png

12. Chlorophyll compound – Adapted from:
    http://en.wikipedia.org/wiki/File:Chlorophyll_a.svg

13. Glyceraldehyde-3-Phosphate figure
    http://en.wikipedia.org/wiki/File:G3P-2D-skeletal.png

14. Cell growth phases – Original

15. Meiosis
    http://en.wikipedia.org/wiki/File:Meiosis_Overview.svg

16. Punnett Square - Original

17. 4x4 Punnett Square - Original

18. DNA nucleotide bases – Adapted from information on structures found in: http://en.wikipedia.org/wiki/File:DNA_chemical_structure.svg

19. Uracil figure
http://en.wikipedia.org/wiki/File:Uracil.svg

20. Codon Table - Adapted from: http://en.wikipedia.org/wiki/DNA_codon_table

21. DNA Operator Adapted from:
http://en.wikipedia.org/wiki/File:Lac_Operon.svg

22. Immune system figure – Adapted from:
http://en.wikipedia.org/wiki/File:Lymphocyte_activation_simple.png

23. Plasmid figure
https://www.clear.rice.edu/bioc111/bios111_day1.htm

24. Phylogenetic tree
http://commons.wikimedia.org/wiki/File:PhylogeneticTree.png

25. Taxonomy figure - Original

26. Greenhouse gas energy reflection figure - Original